DO YOU LOVE ME?

THE ASTROLOGY OF RELATIONSHIPS

JOHN GREEN

MISPA

MISPA BOOKS

1. DICK CLEGG

Manager of the England Angling Team

DICK CLEGG was born at Hoyland Common, to Charles and Mary, on 1 May 1938. He started to fish as a young boy of about eight years old at places such as Rockingham Colliery Pond and Worsbrough Dam, anywhere that was within walking or cycling distance. His father used to accompany him, more as an occasional hobby, than as a regular one. Angling was a typical outdoor pursuit, even more so in those days, because there were no other distractions that would keep young boys indoors, such as television or computers. Dick's school days were spent at Hoyland Common Infant and Juniors, followed by Holgate Grammar School.

Dick's first job upon leaving school was at Samuel Fox's, Stocksbridge. He stayed there for five years, and then took up fresh employment at a firm in Sheffield, the Industrial Furnace Design Company based at an old war-time army barracks at Hillsborough. Dick was an engineer. He was married by then, and when Dick was in his late twenties, he and his father and brother David, bought a fishing tackle shop. The shop was in Huddersfield, and Dick's wife Nanette ran it. Eventually, the business expanded into more shops, including one in Barnsley, and now Dick has an industrial unit down Pontefract Road, manufacturing fishing tackle.

Long before this however, a fishing team was established in the Barnsley area. The name came from a germ of an idea by Tony Wilson, Dennis White and Alan Sefton, all well-known Barnsley anglers. They, along with Harry Jackson from Stockport, fished their first match on the River Trent at Dunham Bridge. I asked about the name, Barnsley Blacks. Dick said that it could have originated because it was a coal mining area, or the use of the larvae of the Blackfly, which Lancastrians said was Yorkshire's favourite. Either way, the name stayed. Several founder members are still in the Barnsley Blacks such as Tom Pickering, Dennis White, and Keith Hobson. Dick Clegg was Captain from the early eighties, interspersed with Tom Pickering, who finally took over. There have been several sponsors over the years, the latest one being Fox International. This is a specialist company that has branched out into angling equipment. It is good for them to have publicity, and it is also of benefit to the team. A lot of the competitions are sponsored by firms such as Embassy and Whitbread. Rich pickings are to be made for a top international angler. In the National Championships, there are five divisions, with a thousand anglers taking part in each division.

Dick is a life-member and delegate of Barnsley and District AAA(Amalgamated Angling Society). This is a federation of anglers of small clubs in the area, and it boasts a thousand members. Dick stressed that if they choose a team for a major match, and that person or team wins, then they are representing the Barnsley AAA, and are fishing for them, not their own team. He added that there have been a few misconceptions about this.The AAA have won First Division Championships twice. They were also reigning champions for 1995 on the Gloucester Canal, and for this reason, they were chosen to fish in the World Club Championships held at Redon, in Brittany, 1996. The squad of seven were Tom Pickering (Captain), Dennis White, Peter Bagshaw, Alan Scotthorne, Simon Roff, Keith Hobson, and Stuart Killen. Unfortunately, they did not win this event.

Dick said that the NFA (National Federation of Anglers), of which Barnsley is a member, organise most of the major championships. They make the selections, and it's on a par with, for example, the Football League. Dick chooses the final squad for the World Championships. Since he took over the job of manager of the England International Team in 1984, they have won the World Championships team competition five times. Six individual gold medals have also been won by Tom Pickering, Dave Roper, Alan Scotthorne and Bob Nudd from Essex, who took three gold medals. This has been during the time that Dick has been in charge.Venues have been at Nottingham, Italy, Portugal, Belgium, and Hungary. Dick has also co-ordinated many other major events abroad, such as Sweden and Denmark, where Tom Pickering broke the world record.

In 1990 Dick Clegg was awarded the MBE (Member of the British Empire) for his services to angling. Basically, Dick said, it was because he was manager of the England Team, and he represented them. They had many achievements, and European anglers were purchasing equipment in a bid to emulate them. This resulted in exports multiplying ten-fold. Dick puts a lot of time and effort into his ventures however, and also many hours unpaid work on behalf of Barnsley, and the NFA. His trip to Buckingham Palace with his wife, was an occasion to be remembered.Travelling early, they arrived at Buckingham Palace and were ushered into the ballroom. Eventually, Dick's name was called, and he walked up to the Queen and shook hands. She asked what the honour was for, and where they fished. A proud moment for Dick.

His favourite kind of angling is river-fishing. A running line with a stick float. Dick thinks that this is the best form of angling ever. He remarked that there are less fishermen than there used to be, because it is so expensive now. There's the equipment, transport, and the cost of tickets on the bank. 'It's rather ironic,' Dick paused, 'in England, the anglers have gone over to the continental style, whilst they have swapped to the British style.' By this, he was referring to the long carbon poles which are quite popular now, in place of the slim rod and line. Dick hasn't got a preference, saying that in match fishing, competition is very fierce, and the long pole is harder to handle. He freely admits though, that on match days, there is a lot of comradeship, with much joking and laughter. This he enjoys, along with the travelling together, and having breakfast with his mates. It helps to gear them up for the competition, which can get quite

Dick Clegg in his office with a few of his trophies.

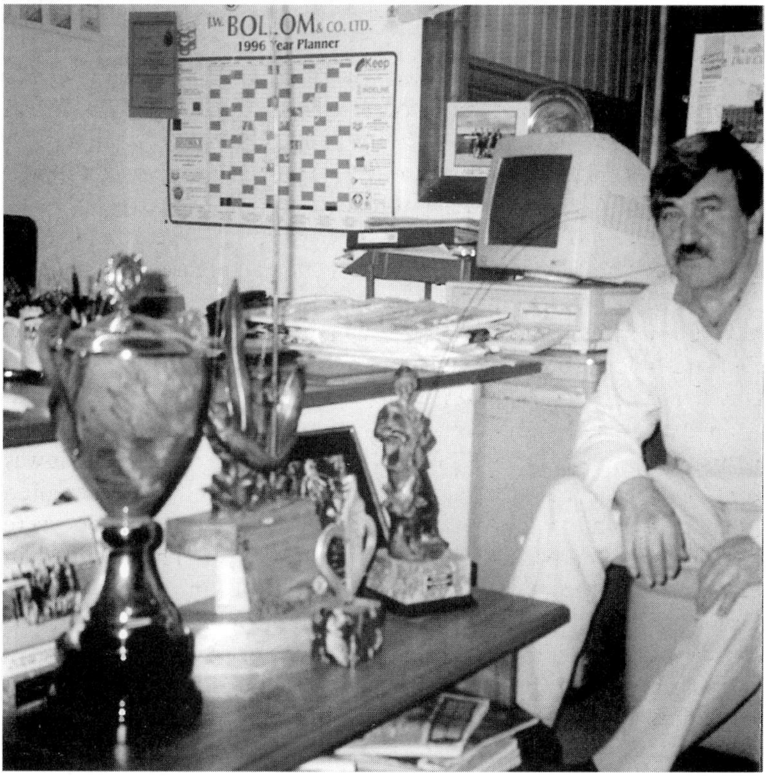

intense. At the end of the day, it is euphoria or deflation, depending upon how the competition went. This can be the luck of the draw, with each angler drawing a number out of the bag, which will decide where his position will be on the bank. As Dick said, 'If you are in an area where the fish don't want to be, then you won't get any. It's a certain amount of luck, the right place at the right time.'

Apart from match fishing, and if the weather is good, Dick remarked that in his youth, one of the joys of pleasure fishing is just being in the country. Sparkling water, a clear blue sky, and all the elements of nature around. 'The kids can enjoy it too,' Dick smiled, 'providing you don't let them fall in.' His own two children were not interested, his son Andrew's hobby is motor racing, and his daughter Catherine, who is an air stewardess, enjoys horse-riding. Dick also enjoys golfing and gardening, when he has the time to fit them in. He is a business man, first and foremost, and because of his keen interest in angling, has been instrumental in helping to create Barnsley's big-match teams. If Dick has his way, long may they flourish.

2. TOM PICKERING

Angling, The Barnsley Blacks Captain

TOM PICKERING took over the captaincy of the angling team, Barnsley Blacks, from Dick Clegg in August 1994, having exchanged the position three times previously and at intermittent intervals with him. He was born at South Kirkby to Audrey and Tom on 12 May 1955. In the Pickering family, the first-born son has always been named Thomas since 1700. When he was a baby, he was taken to Leeds with his parents, but after a year, they both went their separate ways, and Audrey returned to South Kirkby. Tom went to the local Infant and Junior schools, and then to Minsthorpe High School. An interesting story emerged twenty years after the split between his parents. They married each other again, Tom being Best Man. As he remarked, there was still something between them. Unfortunately, they were not together for long, before his mother sadly died of leukaemia. The story did not finish there, it transpired that Tom, who already had a sister, Julie, acquired another in 1995, from a relationship which his father had many years ago. Her name was Jill. She had been told that her father was dead, but she tracked him down, and Tom said that the family were staggered at these happenings.

When Tom was six, his uncle used to take him fishing, and this kindled his interest. As he grew up, he became obsessed with fishing and picked up many tips from the older men. It was obvious that Tom had a special talent and in time he was beating the same men in match-fishing, who had previously taught him. He would practise as much as possible, usually at South Kirkby Colliery Pond. During school holidays, he would be there every day from dawn to dusk. Sometimes he would cycle to Wintersett Reservoir at Ryhill for a change, and to broaden his experience. He was looking for someone who was as keen on angling as he. When he was sixteen, he met Dennis White and formed a friendship which is still in force today. The first match that Tom won, was instigated by Mill Lane WMC. It was their annual event, and his catch weighed 1lb 14ozs. He also won his first open match for the Tadcaster Rose Bowl, on the River Derwent at Stamford Bridge. When Tom was sixteen, he applied to join Doncaster and District AAA, but was not successful, so Dennis suggested that he try for the Barnsley branch. By this time, Tom had a good club record, and was accepted. A year after, the Barnsley Blacks team were started, with Tom and Dennis becoming founder members. A Winter League Table was formed, and in 1976, they won. Since then, they have travelled the length and breadth of Britain,winning numerous prizes. They have also represented Barnsley and District AAA in the World Club Championships. Tom himself broke the World Record in a match at Skanderburg, Denmark with a catch of 323lbs 11ozs.

The Barnsley Team winning the Embassy Division One National Angling Championship in 1995, Left to right: Back row Tim Hannah, Dick Clegg, Dave Clarkson, Keith Hobson, Tony Peel, Dave Chatterton, Pete Bagshaw, Tony Wood, Tom Pickering, Stewart Killen, Dave Nicholson, Simon Roff, Alan Scotthorne, Bob Bell. Front row Wayne Bartholomew, Malcolm Burdett, Dennis White, Alan Taylor, Andy Kinder, Mick Vials.

Victors of the 1995 Embassy Challenge held in Denmark, Left to right:Dennis White, Pete Mansey, Tom Pickering.

There are up to twenty anglers allowed into the club, Tom would not allow any more. 'We have a nucleus of young anglers, who are very good,' he added, 'everybody wants to beat the Barnsley Blacks. We have an excellent squad, and carry a lot of prestige.' Tom had worked at Frickley Colliery from leaving school, then he and his wife, Ann, decided to buy a shop in Doncaster, selling fishing tackle. It had already existed for thirty years, so it was a sound business to take over. However, after twelve years, they have sold up and moved into a wholesale unit.

Ann is an angler in her own right, representing England in international matches. She and Tom have won the Jack Purchase mixed pairs together. She would like to fish more, but family commitments make it impossible. They have two young children, Thomas, who loves football, and Emma, who is mad on fishing, like her parents. Tom remarked that in the last five years, angling has changed beyond recognition, due mainly to technology. Better equipment, rods, reels, and lines. The type of fishing has changed too, the biggest aspect being pole fishing, up to seventeen metres long. It doesn't bother Tom which method he uses, the pole, or the traditional rod and line. He is open-minded, and likes the variety of both methods. I mentioned that patience must be a virtue when it comes to fishing. 'Not really,' he laughed, 'I've known a few people without it, but they can still catch fish.' Tom believes that angling should be left as uncomplicated as possible. He only match-fishes in fresh water, because of the deterioration of some rivers. Mainly, he goes to ponds, lakes, and canals. One of the pleasures that Tom enjoys about angling, is the environment. Being at one with nature. His friend Dennis, coaches youngsters, and this is one subject that he teaches them to be aware of. Catching fish is a bonus, and they should really appreciate their surroundings. Young Emma is fortunate to have parents who are top anglers, and she may follow in their footsteps. But above all, both children come from a sports-loving family, and I am sure will be encouraged in every way.

Tom has now resigned as Captain of the Barnsley Blacks, succeeded by Tony Peel.

3. RONALD BEVERLEY

1921-1985

Kingstone Angler

RONALD BEVERLEY, OR 'MICK' as he was known by fellow Kingstoner's, was born on 17 March 1921 (St Patrick's Day), at 3 Upper Sykes Street. His story was related to me by his niece, Pauline, born 23 April 1937 (St George's Day), and incidentally, my close friend for the last sixty years. The mix-up with Mick's name occurred, because his mother, Anne, had him registered as Ronald, against his father, William's wishes. He insisted on calling him Mick, so henceforth everyone knew him by that name. Mick attended Racecommon Road School until he was fourteen, leaving to go down the mines. His first pit was Levitt Hagg at Hood Green where he worked with his brother Jack, Pauline's father. Following this came Rob Royd, where he trained to be a road ligger and salvager, and finally, Dodworth Colliery, where he spent the last of his working days.

As a youngster, he was interested in many sports besides angling, one of these being knur and spell. He would compete against Amos Eastwood, Frank Raynes Lenthall, and other mates from Kingstone. They used to practise in a field off Dark Lane, between Portman's and Clarke's farms. His other love was football, playing for Kingstone United. The pitch was known as the 'Bull Fields' on Broadway. Mick's younger brother, Frank, also played. Pauline, her sister Beryl, and I, have spent many happy hours as children playing in these same fields and country lanes.

On 21 August 1942, Mick married his sweetheart, Violet Rowntree, a local girl. It was during the war, and Violet was in the ATS. They consequently took up residence at 3, Court Yard One, known locally as Cut-Throat-Yard. It was a small terrace, with no back door. Because Mick was a miner, and it was classed as an essential occupation, he could not join the military services, so he did the next best thing, becoming an APR (Auxilliary Personal Rescue) Warden in the Fire Service for the Home Guard. He liked to relate how he got the job of being in charge. One of the questions was, how would he approach a child in a cot, in a corner of a burning room, if there was a fire in the room below. Mick's answer was that he would skirt around the edge, because the middle would be the weakest

'That's the way to do it.' Ron Beverley pictured with his bumper catch of fish weighing 133lbs. Taken in June 1968.

point. He was given the job but, became most despondent when he realised that his men were enjoying a pint in Kingstone Club at the weekends, and he could not desert his post. One Saturday, he decided to join them, but there was an inspection of the post, and he was court-martialled for desertion. 'Funnily enough,' Pauline said,'he wasn't too upset.'

Shortly after they were married, Violet became pregnant, so had to leave the ATS. They eventually had two children, Ronald and Vera, so obviously Ron did not object to his real name being used. He was a small, wiry man, as indeed were all his brothers, Tom, Jack, and Frank. He also had three sisters, Emily, May and Minnie. Violet said that for his size, he had a large appetite. After a huge dinner each day, he would follow with two slices of thick toast without fail. Astonishingly, he never put an extra ounce on his small frame, and Pauline said that he was classed as a thoroughbred. The family eventually became rehoused in a brand new house at Athersley, three bedrooms, bathroom, toilet, and gardens. This was luxury compared to their previous residence.

Mick was a founder member of Athersley Social Club on Mansfield Road. He took his hobbies, snooker and fishing seriously, putting a great deal of effort into both. He won many prizes and cups. He also bought himself a motor-bike, to take him to his sports events, later changing to a Reliant Robin. One day, in 1968, he weighed in a record catch at Nostell Priory. Here are his own words, taken from a letter:

ON MONDAY, June 17, I had a bumper catch of tench to the tune of 133 lbs. It was opening day on this particular water, as there is no Sunday fishing. It was the first time I had fished this water, as I had only made myself a member this year. It cost me 25 shillings for a permit, and 9s and 8d to be a member of Nostell Working Men's Club, whose water it is. This Nostell Priory Dam is about five miles from Wakefield on the main Wakefield-Doncaster Road.

The swim I had chosen, had not been pre-baited, although my friend and I had dragged two swims out the previous Friday. I was down at the dam by 2am, and took with me one stone of sharps, one stone of bran, ten pounds of bread crumbs, and 10s worth of maggots, plus one pint of pinkies which I got from Steve Calcott of Sheffield.

I put a fair amount of ground bait in before daylight broke, and started fishing around 4am. I was into 2lb tench practically straight away. I was fishing with a rod I had made myself, and was using an Alcocks match aerial centre pin reel loaded with 5lbs breaking strain Bayer line, a number 12 hook (spade end) tied direct to line; a float which I had made myself out of a piece of cane and with a balsa

The triumphant Athersley Social WMC Coronation Cup-winning team, presented at the Barnsley Amalgamated Angling Association dinner held at Worsbrough Welfare Hall, Left to right: Raymond Hawkins, Ron Beverley, Stan Pychowski, George Greenwood, and their wives.

body - this carried four number two shots - and I was fishing with five maggots on the hook. I was still catching the odd fish when I packed up at 3pm, and all the fish weighed between 2 and 3lbs.

I went again the following day, and I fished in the next swim to the one I had caught all the fish - there was someone in this one - and I had 54 tench all around the same weight as the day before. It was the very best two days I have ever had. I had my first catch witnessed by two individual witnesses. The following year, Mick again gained recognition for his fishing in the same place, Nostell Priory, and again on opening day. He weighed in again with a catch of 127lbs of perch, fully witnessed by two other anglers. He said at the time, 'It's no comfort to stand in the water all day, but who cares when you are catching fish like these.' The following Thursday, he again took a good weight of 30 tench, totalling 80lbs.

In 1983, Mick contracted cancer of the stomach. He had an operation at Barnsley General Hospital, but was still in pain afterwards. He was however, determined that it would not change his life, and he bravely carried on with his fishing and snooker to the very last. In September 1985, he drove to Hunstanton, King's Lynn, where his brother Tom had a caravan. They would use this as a base for their fishing trips. Sadly, Mick passed away in his sleep in the caravan on 30 October, he was 64. Mick Beverley had enjoyed a full and active life. He gained a great deal of pleasure from his chosen sports, especially fishing, because as most miners will agree, an outdoor hobby is a bonus, and Mick took full advantage of the open air, and everything it had to offer.

Raymond Hawkins and Ron Beverley admiring the day's catch.

4. DOROTHY HYMAN

Double Olympic Medalist and 'World's fastest Woman'

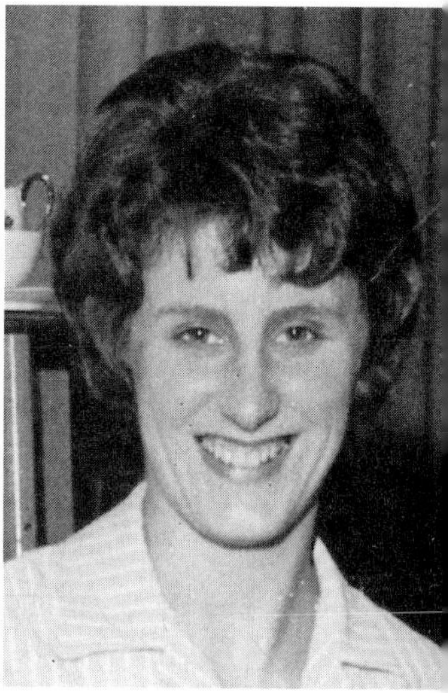

MISS DOROTHY HYMAN found fame throughout the world as an international athlete and Olympic medalist and is a highly respected and well-liked person in the Barnsley area. She was the very first sports' star that I interviewed, so it was with some trepidation that I approached her. My fears were groundless however, as she welcomed me into her home at Stairfoot. It had an air of quiet contentment, reflected in Dorothy herself. Settling myself down in her comfortable armchair, I began by asking whether her parents had originated from Barnsley. 'Well mum was', she replied, 'but dad came from Walsingham in Norfolk. Father's family originally came to Royston, and then settled in Cudworth where he met my mum'.

Her father's name was Albert John, but everyone called him 'Jack'. Her mother's name was Kathleen Cullen, but she was known as 'Kitty' or Kate. Kathleen's grandparents were Irish so she was given a very traditional name of that country in honour of her forbears. The eldest in Jack's family was his brother Charlie, who was a survivor of twins. He was followed by Bill, then Jack, Gladys, and another boy, Harold. Dorothy's paternal grandfather died young and her grandmother remarried. This was followed by the birth of another three children.

When Dorothy was born on 9 May 1941, her parents Jack and Kate had recently moved to 63 Bloemfontein Street, Cudworth. This was the family home until she reached the age of twenty, then they moved into a council house nearby. It was from the first home that Dorothy started school, Snydale Road Infants, Pontefract Road Juniors, and then the Senior school, Cudworth Secondary Modern.It was here that Dorothy's athletic potential was discovered. Her father at that time was her greatest encouragement. She was around twelve or thirteen when her training started. At this age Dorothy ran an 80 yard sprint race and won a chrome dish for her efforts.

Dorothy's father spent many long hours coaching her in Carlton Fields, close to the back of Cudworth Park. Jack had bought his

Dorothy at ease wearing her Commonwealth Games blazer.

daughter her very first pair of spiked running shoes after her initial win. Dorothy treasured them. Unfortunately, you don't have starting blocks in the middle of a field that people are walking on the whole time, so Dorothy had to make do with holes roughly hewn out of the ground to give her a good starting position. It was at this time, when she was still thirteen, that Eddie Fleetwood, the second team coach for Barnsley Football Club, had seen how fast Dorothy could run, and volunteered to coach her himself. He introduced her to the Oakwell ground and it became quite a good training venue for her. At the age of fourteen, Dorothy joined Hickleton Main Youth Club where she remained a member until her retirement.

Dorothy Hyman's earlier competitions were in handicap races. These were usually part of some kind of local sports or gala, organised, for example, by the police, the Coal Board, or the Co-op. The prizes would usually be fruit spoons, vases etc, and in some cases, medals. Because of Dorothy's developing skills however, more often than not, she was handicapped by being made into the back marker. This gave Dorothy an added spur, and in the end admitted, 'It was good experience'. The races usually started on Saturdays in early May and would carry on through the summer until August.

Alongside these events would be the Yorkshire Championships, the Nationals, and the Northern Championships.

The first big event for Dorothy was racing in the Yorkshire Junior Championship at Leeds, 2 June 1956. She came first in the 100 yards sprint in an excellent time of 11.9 seconds. This led to her appearing in Plymouth on 20 July 1956, in the All-England Schools Junior Championships. Again, Dorothy came first, in an even faster time of 11.5 seconds. Being away from home at this time at such a young age, Dorothy found it rather unsettling. However, winning a medal helped to make up for it. This was also her last year as a junior, the following year she moved into intermediate status.

On 6 July 1957, at the White City Stadium in London, Dorothy ran in the WAAA Intermediate Championships. This particular race stands out in Dorothy's memory because she had such a resounding victory. She came first again in the one hundred with a time of 10.9 seconds, but won convincingly, by five yards. This result meant that Dorothy was promoted to international level at the ripe old age of sixteen, a great achievement. Dorothy's career was strictly amateur, not professional. The only money that she earned was from the jobs she had when she left school. Her first was working at a factory, machine-sewing underwear for Marks and Spencer. The second was working as a tracer in the offices of the National Coal Board at Woolley Colliery. Jack used to run her around in his old Hillman Minx. Dorothy was one of five children, the others being Ann, John, David and Susan, so there was never a lot of money to spare, though

Having a well-earned rest!

there was always good food on the table.

Dorothy Hyman's first international appearance was at the White City Stadium, Great Britain versus France, on 3 August 1957. She came third in this event with a time of 11.9 seconds over a hundred yards, and with a strong headwind. She was narrowly beaten by Heather Young who recorded 11.4 seconds. At that time Dorothy was in awe at racing with such a famous athlete. In 1958 she was actually teamed for the first time with Heather, Madeleine Weston, and June Paul, in the 4 by 110 yards relay at the Empire and Commonwealth Games, held at Cardiff on 26 July 1958. They came first with a time of 45.3 seconds, creating a new world record. It was at this time that Dorothy took a new coach. His name was Dennis Watts. It was mainly on an advisory basis, because Dennis lived near Liverpool. Her father still encouraged her, and contact was never lost with Eddie Fleetwood, who by then had been coaching Dorothy for five years.

In 1960 Dorothy Hyman represented Great Britain at the Rome Olympics. She entered her first heat of 100 metres on 1 September, qualifying comfortably by coming first with a time of 11.8 seconds.

Happy neighbours giving Dorothy a hero's welcome and placing a gold locket around her neck after her 1960 Olympics triumph.

Dorothy showing off her Olympic medals to her very proud mum in 1960.

The second round on the same day saw her win again in 11.6 seconds. In the semi-final, held the day after, she won again in 11.5 seconds, and finally, on 2 September at 4pm came the main event itself. Wilma Rudolph of the United States of America won the race and a gold medal with a time of 11.0 seconds. Dorothy completed in 11.3 seconds, taking second place and winning the silver medal. She was disappointed at not achieving gold, but very thrilled to come second in the greatest women's sprint event in the world. It was a heart-stopping moment for her in the Rome sunshine, a moment to cherish, and an honour for Britain.

A further race was to follow, the 200 metres. Dorothy came third in the final, held on 5 September. She took the bronze medal with a time of 24.7 seconds. Wilma Rudolph again won the gold in 24.00 seconds, followed by Jutta Heine of Germany who took the silver with a time of 24.4. Two medals for Dorothy was a great achievement.

In 1963 Dorothy was made captain of the British women's team. This resulted in wins over Germany, America, the Netherlands, Russia, and Hungary. Dorothy was so popular that television viewers voted her the BBC Sports Personality of 1963 in the Television Theatre, West London. She was acclaimed as Britain's 'golden girl'.

The next major event for Dorothy was in 1964 when she was again chosen for the Olympics, this time to be held in Tokyo. On 16 October, Dorothy reached the final of the 100 metres, but came 8th with a time of 11.9 seconds. In the 200 metres she failed to qualify. It must be said though, that if Dorothy had equalled her European record she would have won the gold medal in the 100 metres quite comfortably, but she was only just recovering from a nagging thigh

Here you are Dorothy, keep your strength up

WAAA Championships, Crystal Palace. 18 July 1969. Dorothy during her 200 metres heat, running for her own club, the Dorothy Hyman Track Club. In the final she won in 23.7 seconds, inside the European Qualifying Standard.

injury sustained a few weeks before. Her mother said that 'Time had been Dorothy's enemy. If the games had been held the year before, or even a fortnight later, then she might well have won the gold medal. As things were, she was not on top form after her injury.'

All was not lost however, because the Great Britain sprint squad of Dorothy, Janet Simpson, Mary Rand, and Daphne Arden, broke the Empire, Commonwealth and United Kingdom National Records with a time of 44.0 seconds in the women's 4 by 100 metres relay. They came third behind Poland and the U.S.A. This gave them their bronze medal.

The fastest times that Dorothy has clocked up have been 100 yards in 10.6 seconds, 100 metres in 11.3 seconds, and 23.2 for 200 metres.

I asked Dorothy about the uniform that was worn when representing Great Britain in the Olympics. I know myself that when I have watched teams marching by on the television, so smartly dressed, then it has been a very heart-stirring sight. She told me that normally, the British team would be dressed in different shades of blue, but in Tokyo she wore a pink dress with a jacket over the top. Rome was pale blue with a red hat. In fact, when Dorothy and her dad set off for the Rome Olympics, they had only got halfway to Doncaster railway station when she realised that THE hat had been forgotten. Poor old dad had to drive all the way back to Cudworth to retrieve it. Not a good start, but eventually the plane was boarded some hours later.

Her homecoming after the 1960 Olympics was quite momentous. The brass bands were playing, and around 15,000 people turned out to cheer her. The date was 12 September 1960. Her return from Tokyo in 1964 was quieter, at Dorothy's request, because she still felt keenly the absence of her father. Jack had died suddenly in 1962, aged 53. Dorothy was absolutely shattered, the man who had endeavoured to put her on the road to fame, and her dear friend, was gone.

Throughout Dorothy's career she has travelled to many far-flung places, amongst them, New York, Tokyo, Rome, Perth, Moscow and Stockholm. I remarked that it must have been pretty wonderful when visiting these countries, but she replied that in her younger years it was not appreciated as much as now, looking back in her maturity. The essence of thought then, was to run her very best and simply come home. Athletes did have leisure time and could go sight-seeing, but in the main they had gone out there to do a job. Also, in hot countries they were told not to overdo the sun.

'But', as she repeated, 'the driving force was to do what we had set out for, and not to be distracted by the place itself, no matter how interesting it may be'.

When Dorothy finished running in 1964, she coached at Hickleton for just over twelve months, and with others formed an athletics club at Cudworth itself.

I asked Dorothy when she had first dreamed of a stadium being built? Her reply was that the idea came from the people of Cudworth. They wanted one to be built in her honour. The money came from a sports' association, local clubs getting together and forming a supporters club. Initially, help from this source came in the form of running shoes with which to help Dorothy. This escalated into a draw. Tickets were circulated throughout Cudworth, and then Barnsley council became involved. Organised loans were sought and in the end came the culmination of everyone's desires, the Dorothy Hyman Stadium. Dorothy herself laid the foundation stone on 10 September 1972, but the building was officially opened by Michael Parkinson on 28 April 1973. Barnsley Metropolitan Borough took over, and lots of facilities were improved. For example, whereas it started off as a cinder track, it now boasts a superb tartan running surface. I asked Dorothy if many athletes had shown promise in the area during this same period in time. She replied that there were quite a few which sprang to mind, amongst them, Val Peat, Denise Ramsden, Sheila Cooper, Linda Barrett and Jocelyn Hoyt-Smith, all County and International runners.

After many years of working for the NCB, Dorothy switched jobs and worked as a home-help organiser. It was a very responsible position though, and she worried about the people in her care. If an employee was ill, then a replacement had to be found quickly, which was sometimes a difficult task. She left this job, and currently works at Monk Bretton, helping people with learning difficulties, and finding the work very rewarding.

Looking back, Dorothy said that certain sacrifices had to be made such as boy friends, dancing and a social life, but she knew that if success in her own field was to be achieved, then she could not have both. Marriage and babies would have been fine, but then she would not have been our Dorothy, a great runner. Her lifestyle has made her the kind of person she is today. Upon reflection, she thought that perhaps retirement was a little premature. If Jack had lived, he might have persuaded his daughter to carry on a little longer. In actual fact, Dorothy took up running again in 1969/70, and at the age of 29 was racing better than ever. A book had been ghost-written about her,

Sprint to Fame, and because money was involved then Dorothy automatically became a professional. There again, if her father had been living, then he could have overseen the book and Dorothy could have retained her amateur status. But as Dorothy commented, 'These were all if's'.

After her retirement, she formed the Dorothy Hyman Track Club. She took up running again, but could no longer enter internationally because of her professional status. However, she coached her squad and helped to bring them up to international standard. The fact that Dorothy was winning races though, led to acrimony between herself and some of her pupils. She found this particularly upsetting after trying to bring out the best in them, and this led to her permanent retirement after the Yorkshire Championships in 1970.

Miss Hyman has represented Great Britain approximately 40 times. She has equalled or broken 19 UK records, 5 European records, and has been a member of relay teams breaking two World records.

As we were nearing the end of the interview, I noticed an embroidered picture on the wall. A copy of a Lowry print. Dorothy had painstakingly done this herself. Another facet of her character which shows that she tackles a job right to the very end. It was an enjoyable meeting, and one on which I shall look back with pleasure.

HIGHLIGHTS OF MISS DOROTHY HYMAN'S CAREER IN WOMEN'S ATHLETICS

1956 – *20 July, Plymouth,* All-England Schools junior championship, 100 yds, 1st, 11.5 – *25 August, Chiswick,* W.A.A.A. junior championship, 100 yds, 1st, 12.0

1957 – *3 August, White City,* G.B. v France, first international for Dorothy, 100 yds, 3rd, 11.9, Young won in 11.4

Empire Games, Cardiff 1958

19 July, first Commonwealth Championships for Dorothy, 100 yds heat, 2nd, 11.0 – *19 July,* semi-final, 100 yds, 4th, 11.1 – *26 July,* 4x110 yds relay, 1st, 46.1 – *26 July,* 4x110 yds relay, 1st, 45.3, a world record. Weston, Hyman, Paul, and Young.

European Championships, Stockholm.

20 August, 100 met, heat, 3rd, 12.0

21 August, 100 met, semi-final, 5th, 12.3

23 August, 4x100 met relay, heat, 3rd, 46.3

24 August, 4x100 met relay, final, 2nd, 46.0. Weston, Hyman, Dew, and Quinton

W.A.A.A. Championships, Motspur Park 1959.

4 July, final, 100 yds, 1st, 10.8

4 July, final, 220 yds, 1st, 24.5, Dorothy's first win for W.A.A.A

Olympic games, Rome 1960
1 September, 1st round, 100 met, 1st, 11.8
1 September, 2nd round, 100 met, 1st, 11.6
2 September, semi-final, 100 met, 1st, 11.5
2 September, final, 100 met, 2nd, 11.3
3 September, 200 met, heat, 1st, 23.7
5 September, 200 met, semi-final, 2nd, 24.6
5 September, 200 met, final, 3rd, 24.7
7September, semi-final, 4x100 met, 1st, 45.8
8 September, final, 4x100 met, disqualified. Quinton, Hyman, Smart, and Bignall.

Dorothy missed some fixtures, due to her father's death, 14 May, 1962.

European Championships, Belgrade, 1962.
12 September, 100 met, heat, 1st, 11.6
13 September, 100 met, semi-final, 1st, 11.6
13 September, 100 met, final, 1st, 11.3
14 September, 200 met, heat, 1st, 23.9
14 September, 200 met, semi-final, 2nd, 23.7
15 September, 200 met, final, 2nd, 23.7
15 September, 4x100 met relay heat, 2nd, 45.4
16 September, 4x100 met relay final, 3rd, 44.9. Packer, Hyman, Arden, and Rand.
This was very special to Dorothy because she won her first major gold medal after her father's death. She won gold, silver, and bronze from these events.

Empire Games, Perth, 1962
24 November, 100 yds, heat, 1st, 11.0
24 November, 100 yds, semi-final, 1st, 10.7
26 November, 100 yds, final, 1st, 11.2
26 November, 220 yds, heat, 2nd, 24.5
26 November, 220 yds, semi-final, 1st, 24.0
29 November, 220 yds, final, 1st, 23.8
1 December, 4+110 yds relay, 2nd, 46.6. Packer, Hyman, Arden, and Moore, who fell but still ran whilst injured.

Volvograd, 1963
28 September, Russia v G.B. 100 met, 1st, 11.5. Equalled U.K.record.
29 September, Russia v G.B. 200 met, 1st, 23.4. Equalled U.K. and European record.

Budapest, 1963
2 October, Hungary v G.B. 100 met, 1st, 11.3. Dorothy's fastest time ever over 100 metres.
3 October, Hungary v G.B. 200 met, 1st, 23.2. Dorothy's fastest time ever over 200 metres.

Tokyo, 1963
13 October, 'Olympic rehearsal' final, 200 met, 1st, 23.6
14 October, 'Olympic rehearsal' final, 100 met, 1st, 11.6

Dorothy was proclaimed as the fastest woman in the world throughout 1963.

Besides receiving the TV Sports Trophy, she was made the Woman Athlete of 1963 by the British Athletics Writer's Association, and Sportswoman of the Year by the *Daily Express*.

Dorothy and myself admiring her many trophies.

5. JOHN MAYOCK

Olympic middle distance runner

JOHN PAUL MAYOCK middle distance runner, was born on 26 October 1970. His parents, Edna and Vincent, live in the Hoyland area, and it was there that John and his brother Gary and sisters, Charlotte and Sharron were raised. John's grandparent's originate from County Mayo, Ireland. They settled in London where Vincent was born but he travelled to Barnsley as a young man to seek work down the mines. He met and married Edna from Wombwell and out of their growing family, two world-class athletes emerged, John and Charlotte (born on 11 December 1973). Both children attended St Helen's Roman Catholic School in Hoyland, and then on to Kirk Balk Comprehensive. Eventually, John finished up at Staffordshire University doing Computer Studies. Charlotte went to Barnsley Technical College and passed an athletic scholarship which enabled her to go to Riverside College, California. She stayed there for two years and then moved on to Louisiana State University, where she still is today. Charlotte is a top athlete sponsored by NIKE.

In the early 1980s, John's mum and aunt worked as receptionists at Hoyland Leisure Centre where Pat Greasby (who has since passed away) worked as a pools' attendant. Pat used to be a Yorkshire Champion at running and suggested to Edna that it might be a good idea for her children to join Rockingham Athletic Club. John and Charlotte agreed to go, and at their respective ages, 12 and 9, began their first training sessions. John said that his sister made a marvellous start, she was an instant success. Within three weeks, and racing against older girls in the 8-11 group, she became the South Yorkshire Champion. It was the winter season when they started to train, and in six months' time Charlotte also notched up the English Championship in the National Cross Country races. 'She kept this title for three years on the trot, this had only happened once before,' John said. As for his own part, he admitted that he had made a very slow start in comparison with Charlotte. John was 26th in the boys' 11-13 race. One of the facets of his personality however, is extreme dedication, and John was no mean slouch when it came to proving himself. A man who greatly encouraged John was his coach, Peter Watson, a former well-known athlete based at the Dorothy Hyman Stadium.

John and Charlotte in training.

At the age of fifteen, John started training with a group run by a Yugoslavian, Maden Vezmar, who lived near to the Mayock household. John was still at the Rockingham club, but he received extra coaching, and because there were faster runners than him in this talented athletic squad, he made really good progress. So much so, that within six months he was ranked third in the United Kingdom (3,000 metres). This was a tremendous leap forward, and a tribute to John's sheer hard work. By 1988 he was running in the junior men's events. One particular weekend he celebrated a double win. The first was at a meeting held at Woodbourne Road Stadium, Sheffield, winning the 3,000 metres with a time of 8mins 45.6secs. The second win was the 1,500 metres in the County Championships held at Cudworth with a time of 3mins 54.3secs.

John was still in higher education at Staffordshire University and doing his athletics training with a national coach who was based there. After a while he felt that he was getting a little stale, so decided to make trips back to Barnsley and train again with his old friend Peter Watson. Peter was coaching Peter Elliott at the time, the former Olympic silver, and Commonwealth gold medallist from Rotherham, and one of John Mayock's heroes. Pete Watson invited John to join his group as pacemaker. This was in 1987, but in 1994 unfortunately, Peter Elliott suffered an injury to his achilles tendon and had to have an operation. This took place in America, but was not a success so Peter travels to the Dorothy Hyman Stadium now in an advisory capacity. John likes to train there, saying that the modern tartan track was far better to race on than the old-fashioned cinder type.

I asked John if there were any sporting events that really stood out in his memory. He mentioned the European Junior Championships, 5,000 metres in 1989, and the World Student Games 5,000 metres held in Sheffield, 1991. He was the World Student Champion at this event, representing Staffordshire University for Britain. Pete Watson chipped in, 'He is the only Briton to achieve it, it's a big honour, the best student in the world.' John added, 'The stadium was packed that day, and the atmosphere was absolutely fantastic.' He also won a bronze medal in 1994 at the Commonwealth Games in Victoria, Canada. The event being the 1,500 metres.

When the Don Valley Stadium has a good crowd, it is John's favourite track. Stafford Borough Council and the university are so proud of him that he was offered a job as Sports Promotions Officer. This involves organising sporting events, giving talks to schoolchildren and finding sponsors.

The biggest highlight of John Mayock's career was to be chosen for the Atlanta Olympics in 1996. He had been a reserve for the 1,500 metres and the 5,000 metres held in Barcelona in 1992. To qualify for Atlanta, he ran at an AAA meeting held at the Alexander Stadium, Birmingham. In the 1,500 metres he beat Andy Keith from Hereford, and Tony Whiteman from Kent with an uplifting win of 3mins 37.03 secs. Both John and his coach Pete were delighted, the great ambition was taking shape.

The opening ceremony took place on 19 July 1996. John's race was scheduled for ten days later. There was a lot of heat and humidity around, not ideal conditions for athletes used to colder weather. The track also was more suited to sprinters. However, John overcame these problems and on 3 August 1996, finished eleventh in the 1,500 metres with a time of 3mins 40.18secs. A wonderful achievement, considering also that he had missed about nine weeks

English Schools International Squad. Charlotte Mayock, fourth girl from left, second row down. Taken late 1980s

training in the winter due to injury. His coach Pete said that he was very proud of John, and that it was a great honour to be even chosen for the Olympics.

Since then, John has come first in a race at a charity event held in Sarajevo, Bosnia, watched by 50,000 spectators. He offered his services to help this war-torn city. The distance was 2,000 metres, and his time was 5mins 00.01secs. 18 February 1997 saw him achieve second place in Moscow, in a 1,500 metres race, clocking 3mins 40.00 secs. February, also, saw John come fourth in a 3,000 metres event held at the Birmingham Indoor Arena. It was an open event, and athletes came from all over the world. The winner was Moses Kiptanui from Kenya. John achieved a new British Record of 7mins 42.4secs. His sister Charlotte ran a mile race in Florida, the same weekend. It was an indoor National Championship event with athletes representing eighteen universities from around the country. She came second, winning a silver medal, and running a personal best of 4mins 37secs.

John and Charlotte possess the will to win, and with their ever improving track records, nothing is impossible.

JOHN MAYOCK: HIGHLIGHTS OF HIS CAREER

Started athlectics at the age of twelve, and joined a local athletics club, Rockingham A.C.
English Schools Champion 3000m Wigan, 1988
English Schools Champion X-C Wadebridge, 1988
European Junior Silver Medallist 5000m Varazdin, 1989
World Student Games Champion 5000m Sheffield, 1991
European Indoor Silver Medallist 3000m Genoa, 1992
Commonwealth Games Bronze Medallist 1500m Victoria, 1994
World Championships S/F 1500m Gothenburg, 1995
AAA Champion 1500m Birmingham, 1995

Personal Bests:

800m	1.48.7	1995	
1500m	3.34.05	1995	
MILE	3.51.87	1995	Britain's number one in three distances
3000m	7.47.00	1995	
	7.46 (indoor)	1995	
5000m	13.27	1992	(rarely runs this distance)

Coaches: P. Watson and P. Elliott (athlete)
Training: 1. Stafford
2. Barnsley (once a week in winter and twice in the spring/summer)
Education: Kirk Balk Comprehensive, Barnsley
Barnsley Sixth Form College
Staffordshire University (Computer Studies)
Employment: Stafford Borough Council and Staffordshire University
(Sports Promotions Officer)

6. CHRISTIAN LINSKEY

Champion Pole Vaulter

CHRISTIAN LINSKEY is a young man dedicated to his sport. He lives in the Locke Park area with his parents, Brian and Jennifer. Christian was born on 14 June 1980, and he has a brother, Karl, two years older. Karl has done some weight-lifting and played basket ball in the past, and Brian, the father, was a wrestler for many years, so there has been an element of sport in the family for a long time. Christian went to Agnes Road Infants, then Longcar Junior School, followed by Holgate Comprehensive.

Christian first realised his potential when he won races at his junior school. There was a girl in his class, Rachel Fox, who's father was a coach, and she asked Christian to come along and practise. He eventually started to train at the Dorothy Hyman Stadium. Trevor Fox, who had taken a coaching exam, asked Christian if he would like to practise for a new event after training for a year. The new event was pole-vaulting. Christian 'jumped' at this, and so training of a different kind began. He wasn't quite ten years old, so had to wait for competition.

This took place in 1993, when Christian entered the Northern County Championships in Derby, and became the record holder with a jump of 3.45 metres. He won all the major events that year. During the summertime, Christian trains at the Dorothy Hyman track twice a week, weight-lifting at the Metrodome or a gymnasium in Thurnscoe. The beginning of October and during the winter months he trains at Thornes Park, and Don Valley stadiums. By the time Christian was fourteen, he represented England in the International Schools Championships. He cleared a height of 4.05 metres. He also won many other awards again, and the 1995 season saw him declared McDonald's Young Athlete of the Year. He was also Top Ranked Under 17 Men's Pole Vaulter in the United Kingdom, with a jump of 4.81 metres. He topped the indoor rankings the following year, 1996, at 4.90 metres.

We spoke about the length of the poles. Christian explained that they are individually catered for, depending upon personal strength and speed. Also, they are made from fibre-glass or carbon fibre. At the moment, his pole is about 16ft long. He once snapped one but said that the worst thing that could happen is doing something called 'stalling out.' This is caused by a lack of speed which means that the athlete falls back onto the runway, and not the mat. He mentioned that to take into the air, the pole has to slide into a metal 'planting'

Christian Linskey leaping skyward to clear in the pole vault: England Team Event at Stoke-on Trent, 1996.

Christian Linskey

1995 Season

Pole Vault Records and Championship Performances

National A.A.A. Indoor Champion and Record Holder
4.60m

International Schools Indoor Champion and Record Holder
(Also selected as the England Team Captain)
4.70m

Northern Counties Champion and Record Holder
4.61m

World Record Holder – 14 Year Old Boy Age Group
4.72m

McDonalds Young Athletes League
'Athlete of the Match'
4.60m

English Schools Champion and Record Holder
4.70m

Represented Great Britain under 20's in the Great Britain v France v Benelux Countries – International in Belfort, France

National A.A.A. Outdoor Champion and Record Holder
4.81m

1996 Season

Northern Counties Indoor Champion and Record Holder
4.90m

United Kingdom Indoor Record Holder – Under 17 Men
4.90m

National A.A.A Indoor Champion and Record Holder
4.70m

Represented Great Britain under 20's in the Great Britain (under 20's) v Great Britain Students v Loughborough Students v England International in Loughborough, England
McDonalds Young Athletes League 'Athlete of the Match'
5.00m

Yorkshire Champion and Record Holder
4.80m

Northern Counties Outdoor Champion and Record Holder
5.00m

English Schools Champion
4.50m

box to keep it steady. Therefore not only does the athlete have to run at speed before the lift-off, he also has to decide the precise moment to place the pole. Christian said that he usually has an eighteen stride run-up, covering about thirty-seven metres. The length is measured out for him so that he knows how far he has got to run. He runs at controllable speed, going faster in the last six strides. Christian paused and smiled, 'It gets very technical.'

At the age of sixteen, Christian Linskey is doing marvellously well. He cleared the qualifying height of 5.10 metres, and took the gold medal at the National AAA Under 20 Championships at Bedford. This gave him the right to represent Great Britain in the Under 20 World Championships in Sydney, Australia. He set off on 9 August 1996. Soaring to a height of 5.15 metres, and achieving a personal best, Christian gained ninth place in the qualifying round of the competition. This placed him in the thirteen man final on 20 August 1996 where the winning clearance was 5.35 metres. Considering that Christian is still well under twenty, and improving, he is in a good position to emulate his hero, Sergey Bubka, the Ukranian world record holder. Christian thinks that Sergey is the best pole-vaulter of all. Now, in his early thirties, Bubka first broke the world record with a vault of 5.94 metres, and he was only twenty at the time. The current world record is 6.14 metres, also set by Bubka.

Christian says that his ambition is to become Olympic Champion. I asked him if he had any girl friends. He gave a grin and replied, 'No time.' I am sure that all the folk in Barnsley will wish Christian Linskey every success in his hopes for the future.

7. PETER WATSON

Sprint Champion and Olympic Coach

PETER WATSON is a well known coach to present, and former runners at the Dorothy Hyman Stadium at Cudworth. He was born at Burton Grange, Lundwood, on 21 January 1934. His parents were Joe and Ethel, Pete being their only child. He loved sport from a very early age, playing football and running for his local school. At the age of twelve, he joined Rotherham Athletic Club. By the time he was fourteen, and running for Littleworth Seniors he was Champion of the Barnsley Schools. At fifteen, Pete started work at a butcher's shop in Sheffield Road, Barnsley. At the same time, he was racing and winning in the Yorkshire Championships. By now he was a member of Bank End Athletic Club, alongside such as Gloria Goldsborough, now Mrs Jackson, and Amos Jones, the brother of Mark, describing both as excellent athletes.

In the Yorkshire Championships, held in Roundhay Park, Leeds, Pete took a gold medal for running the 100 yards. Two years later, when he was seventeen, he again won the gold medal in the under-twenties race for the same event. At eighteen, he received his call-up papers and joined the Royal Air Force. Upon leaving at twenty-one, his next employment was in the Fire Service where he stayed for thirty years. Fighting fires however, was not enough for Pete, and he continued with his athletic career by running for the Fire Service. After a while, he stopped racing and took up coaching. Meanwhile, he had married a lady named Ethel, and they were raising three sons, Gary, and twins, John and Alan.

The boys were interested in athletics, so Pete encouraged them by taking up running again when he himself was at the age of thirty-nine. In fact, in later years when his son John was twenty-four, they raced together in a relay. Shortly before Pete was to retire as a fireman, he entered the European Fire Services Athletics Championships at Gateshead. Pete was British coach and team manager. Six nations competed, Britain, Germany, Holland, Ireland, Belgium and France. In the veterans' race, Pete should have appeared in the over fifties, but instead he opted for the over forty-five's and gained a resounding victory. The 100 metres race was held in the face of a very strong headwind, but Pete notched up 12.1

seconds. This result was 1.2 seconds faster than the winner of the over forties section, a tremendous achievement. Pete also entered the veteran's race held at Meadowbank in Scotland. This too was for the over fifties, and Pete succeeded in winning four titles in two days. Representing the United Kingdom, he won the 100 metres, and the

Gloria Goldsborough and Peter in training together, 1984.

Peter pictured with John Mayock and Rotherham's Olympic Champion, Peter Elliott, at the Dorothy Hyman Stadium, 1996.

200 metres, taking gold medals along the way, and then the long-jump, and the triple-jump; and another two gold medals to add to the collection. Pete added that this was one of his proudest moments.

In 1984, Pete ran in another Veteran's race. This time it was at Brighton, and he represented Great Britain in the European Championships. The race was the 4x100 metres relay, where again the team were victorious and received gold medals.

Pete's professional coaching career has taken him all over the world. His sons did not take their ambitions any further, and one of them settled in Lisarow in Australia. Pete regularly visits during the winter, and he is as well-known there for his coaching abilities as in England. His wife Ethel used to accompany him, but sadly, she passed away in May, 1995. Pete has recently re-married an old student friend of her's, Evelyn Mary, who welcomed me into their home at Lundwood.

Pete no longer runs, he just does pure coaching. Neither does he draw a salary, he has great ambitions for other athletes and coaches for the love of it. At one time he had a squad of 160-180 trainee runners, now it's down to 14 girls aged between 15 and 17, but two of them are top internationals and Pete is very proud of them. He has worked with all the top football managers, including Barnsley, training players on a one to one basis. Alan Clarke, Norman Rimmington and Bobby Collins are amongst trainers who have sent people to him. Rotherham too have called upon his services. Also in the past, he has helped with Dorothy Hyman, a good friend. I asked Pete who had been instrumental in training him in his younger days. He replied that it was a man named Herbert Smillie, a former Yorkshire and Northern County Champion. Peter Watson is best known for coaching middle-distance runner, Peter Elliott, the former 1988 Olympic silver medallist and 1990 Commonwealth Games champion. He injured himself in 1994 and now helps Pete in an advisory capacity with 1996 Olympics runner, John Mayock. Between them, they are hoping to foster some great runners at the Dorothy Hyman Stadium. As Pete said, 'The name of the game is dedication, along with natural ability.' Pete is a very good judge of potential athletes, and if any youngster is a budding champion, then he is the right person to nurture and encourage them in their ambition.

8. GLORIA GOLDSBOROUGH

International and Veteran Athlete

GLORIA JACKSON, maiden name, Goldsborough will be remembered very well for her athletic prowess in the 1950s. She was one of Barnsley's foremost runners. Gloria was born on 11 December 1933, to Emma and Clifford at 57 Spring Street, Barnsley. She has a sister, Hazel. Gloria's education started at Agnes Road School, finishing at Rockingham College, where she gained a teaching certificate. She has also been a Youth and Community worker and college lecturer. However, Gloria's first childhood race, which she won, was held at Ardsley Welfare Park when she was eight years old. Her prize was a book or half-a-crown. Gloria chose the book. When she was eleven, her mother entered her into a race which she herself had won at the same age. It was the eighty yard sprint at a Sports Day held in the grounds of Stainborough Park. Gloria followed in her mother's footsteps and won that too.

Running was definitely in the family since Gloria had two uncles from her mother's side of the family who were former athletes: George Porter and Charles Lee. They would both take her training at Locke Park, which entailed running around the bandstand. Sometimes, Charles would mark out a 100 yard run for her down Rockley Lane. At other times, Gloria would wait until the cricket finished at Shaw Lane, and then use these grounds. Of course there were no sponsors in those days, as athletics were strictly amateur, athletes providing their own strip and any equipment. If you were in the England or Great Britain team, then you were provided with a vest. Uncle Charles was in his seventies, but would always pace Gloria. She used to give him about twenty yards start. One day, the police came to her parents' home saying that they had received a phone call stating that a girl was being chased down the road by a man. Fortunately, the police guessed that it would be Gloria because they had seen her in training. This same uncle played football in Locke Park cricket field until he was well into his eighties. On Charles's eightieth birthday, a reporter from a national newspaper went along and took a photograph for their sports page showing Charles and Gloria sprinting.

In the course of time, Gloria took her athletics career seriously

Gloria and Uncle Charles sprinting on his eightieth birthday.

and joined Bank End Athletic Club. She was about fifteen at the time. Other excellent athletes who trained with her were Amos Jones, Peter Watson, Herbert Smillie and her friend, Joan Stocks, who was a half-miler and Gloria's pace-maker. She also trained two nights a week at Barnsley Football Ground with Eddie Fleetwood coaching her. In Gloria's words, 'Eddie was a lovely person with a very calming influence. If ever I lost a race, he used to say, 'Never mind, lass, we'll do it next time.' Gloria competed every Saturday throughout the season, all the races being handicapped. She ran off the back mark, giving up to fourteen yards' start in the 100 yards, and twenty four yards' start in the 220 yards, so she was very fortunate if she won a prize. There were only three sports meetings a year where they all began from scratch, apart from the championships. Another very helpful member was Dennis Senior. He belonged to a boxing and wrestling club which used the facilities of Bank End. He was interested in athletics and used to chauffeur Gloria, her father, and Eddie to major events and championships, otherwise they would have had to use public transport.

Gloria said that there were lots of good local athletes at Bank End Club, so they were able to get some good relay teams together. They were always amongst the medal winners and became so well-known that at the yearly sports meeting, international athletes were attracted. It was the only club Gloria remarked, that had a track large enough to sustain a straight 220 yards. Also, it was a very friendly club and had lots of supporters. On sports days, around 3,000 spectators would usually turn up. Gloria worked in the General Office of the David Brown Company at Penistone, and when eventually Bank End AC closed, David Brown's affiliated to the AAA so Gloria represented them for seven happy years. There were around thirty-five good sprinters in her day, and in her age group, so

Gloria winning the British 440 yards Championship.

it was difficult to make it into the British team. However, Gloria became an international runner in 1953. In the British Championships, held in 1954 at the White City Stadium, London, Gloria ran the fastest time by any woman athlete for twenty-six years: 440 yards in 57.1secs. For this, and other runs of 440 yards in the same year, she was third in the World rankings. In the Yorkshire Championships for 100, 220 and 440 yards she won 10 gold, and 2

Gloria pictured on the winner's rostrum at Tel Aviv in 1956

silver medals. In the Northern Counties Championships, 100, 220, and 440 yards, again, 10 gold, and 2 silver medals. Two gold medals in Holland for the 100 yards, (11.00secs), and 220 yards, (25.2secs). In Israel, when Gloria was twenty, she won 2 gold medals. The first for the 100 yards (10.9secs) and the second for 220 yards (25.1secs).

In 1984, Gloria ran in the European Veterans Championships, taking the gold medal in the 100 metres in 13.8secs and the silver medal in the 200 metres in 28.7secs, a sure sign that the old magic was still there. In all, Gloria Goldsborough held sixteen British titles, including the Veterans. Of all the races that she has taken part in, her most memorable was against the former Olympic champion, Fanny Blankers-Koen of Holland. Blankers-Koen had won four gold medals in the 1948 Olympics. Gloria was racing against her at Hull on a very bumpy grass track. This six-foot tall, elegant athlete strolled over, and Gloria, who was sixteen at the time, said that they were all quaking in their shoes. In the 100 yards heat, Gloria clocked 10.9secs. This had been the fastest time, but in the final, she was pipped at the post by Fanny. Gloria said that it was one occasion when she didn't mind coming second, because she was such a great admirer of hers. Afterwards, in the changing room, Fanny went up to Gloria and said, 'You scared me in the heats, I thought you were going to beat me. Congratulations on a fine race.' They had a long chat together and Gloria remarked that she was one of the nicest persons that she had ever met. Unfortunately, during the 1950s there were no 440 yards, middle or long distance events in the Olympic Games. They were considered to be too strenuous for women. After international athletic meetings held in London, Gloria mentioned that it was usual to be invited to a reception sponsored by a national newspaper. The grandest of all was when she and her fellow athletes were invited to the Dorchester for a seven course dinner, and each received a gift afterwards.

Gloria became Mrs Jackson in 1956 when she married Ivor. They have two daughters, Andrea and Elizabeth, and three grandsons, Christopher, Michael and Mark. Chris, aged fifteen, prefers music to sport, playing classical guitar. He attends Easingwold School, North Yorkshire. Michael and Mark are both sports mad and play Ice Hockey. Michael plays for the Sheffield under-tens team, and both play in the Sheffield House Leagues. Michael has also won several medals for swimming. They both attend Thorpe Hesley School. As for Gloria, she is still interested in most sports, and enjoys watching the Sheffield Steelers ice hockey team.

I enjoyed chatting to Gloria at her home in Worsbrough. She

praised Keith Lodge of the *Barnsley Chronicle*, and John Uprichard of the *Sheffield Star*, stating that in her opinion, they were two of the best sports reporters in Yorkshire, and did much to promote local athletes by their enthusiastic sports columns. I can understand how she was able to win the Veterans race, because she still looks young and fit. Our afternoon passed swiftly, and it was good to listen to Gloria's sporting memories.

Gloria as she is today.

9. ANGELA THORP

Olympic Hurdler

BARBARA AND DEREK THORP, parents of Olympic hurdler Angela Caroline Thorp, warmly welcomed me into their home in Wilson Street, Wombwell, to interview their famous daughter born on 7 December 1972. She has two older brothers, Andrew and Stewart. Angela first became interested in athletics whilst at Wombwell High School. She ran in team events for the school, and eventually joined Wombwell Athletics Club based at the Dorothy Hyman Track, Station Road, Wombwell, staying there until she was eighteen. Two of her school-friends, Paula Burgess and Vanessa Burgess also joined. It was here that Angela won her first race. It was a cinder track, and she was placed in the position next to a high wall, which she found to be a bit intimidating, but nevertheless she went ahead and was successful. She was thirteen at the time and was very thrilled to receive a small plaque for her efforts. Jeannette Tomlin was the coach. Angela wanted to hurdle so Jeannette took her to the Dorothy Hyman Stadium at Cudworth where her potential was spotted by a coach named Audrey Blunt, who took Angela under her wing.

Eventually, Angela was representing Yorkshire in the UK Championships. She said that actually she was a junior when she ran at Cardiff, Wales, in the senior races. Audrey, who travelled to Cudworth from York each week, coached Angela from the age of thirteen to twenty-one, and was a source of inspiration. 'In fact', Angela said, 'she was like a grandma to me, buying Christmas and birthday presents.' Angela moved on to Barnsley Sixth Form College at seventeen and studied sport.

Whilst at college, she took a part-time Saturday job at H Samuels, jewellers, in Barnsley. Upon leaving her college she was offered a full-time post at Abbey National Building Society, where she stayed for around seven years. Starting from 1994 however, Angela received numerous setbacks, and it was touch-and-go as to whether she would gain a place in the Olympics which were to be held in Atlanta, in 1996. Angela had glandular fever, followed by rubella. Recovering from these, an injury was then suffered to her left knee in 1995. This was followed by an operation to release a trapped nerve. The operation was a success, but Angela could not do any training from

September 1995 until March 1996. She felt very helpless during this period and was anxious to resume her career. Angela was not in good shape when training began throughout the month of April, but she entered her first race in May 1996. It was held at Watford and Angela came first in the 100 metres hurdle, beating Clova Court in a time of 13.4 seconds. By now, Angela was training at the Don Valley Stadium, Sheffield, because Audrey Blunt could help her no further. Her coach there was Lewis Samuel, a former 400 metres European Championship sprinter. He was not a hurdler, but he concentrated on Angela's speed. This resulted in her clocking 11.48 seconds in the 100 metres sprint at Birmingham's Alexander Stadium. She was running for Wigan at a National League meeting, but the big trial was yet to come. Again at the same stadium, the AAA meeting was held to determine who would represent England in the Olympics. With a successful timing of 13.26 seconds, Angela was selected. The next stop, Atlanta.

The English squad were flown to Florida two weeks before the Olympic games so that they could acclimatise themselves. The temperature was hot and humid. Angela remarked that they had

Angela Thorpe, a blur of speed.

filled their leisure time by shopping or going to the pictures.She also said that the women's British uniform was very smart, it was a checked dress and jacket. The athletes' sports' clothes were red, white and blue lycra, and tee-shirts. Her parents were not on hand to watch because by the time that it was known that Angela would run in the Olympics, July 1996, it was too late to purchase a ticket for that particular day. Her mum's sister, who lives in Florida was very disappointed too. It was a great thrill for them though, to know that their niece had struggled through illness, and was still good enough to be chosen to represent Britain.

When Angela first stepped onto the track, the magnitude of the crowd overwhelmed her and she had to retreat. She calmed herself down, took a deep breath, and the second time she didn't glance around and felt much better. She said that basically she likes an audience, but at the local events she knows everyone and it's easier. In the first round of the 100 metres hurdles, Angela's time was 12.93 seconds. The second round, held later in the day, gave her a time of 12.99 seconds. She was racing against a formidable hurdler, Gail Devers, an American champion who had previously won the Olympic 100 metres, and was in great form. Angela was through to the semi-final having come second to the American, and with a time of 12.99 seconds. July 31 dawned and the next stage along with it.

Angela displays the uniform worn at the 1996 Atlanta Olympics.

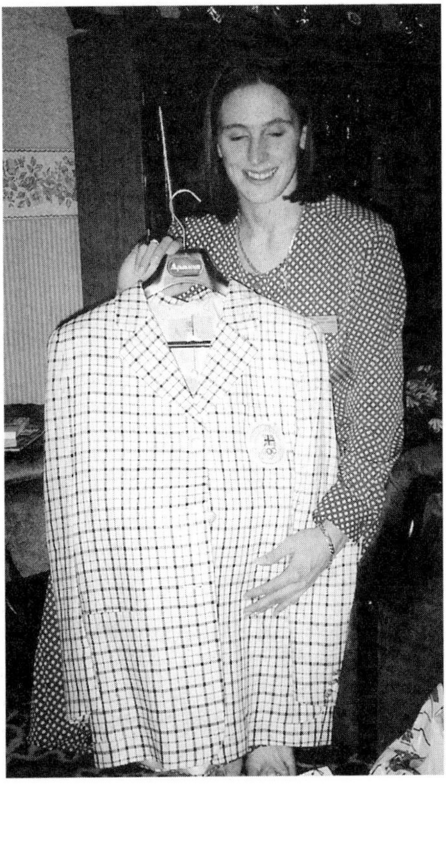

After two false starts, neither of them being Angela's, the race got under way. At the third hurdle, she lay in seventh position, but racing steadily she gained ground and improved to fifth position, missing the fourth place by a hairbreadth. All was not lost however, because she clocked an outstanding personal best of 12.80 seconds, breaking the eight-year old British Record of 12.82 seconds previously held by Sally Gunnell. No medal, but what a proud moment for Barnsley's Angela Thorp. 'When Tony Ward, the Press Officer for the British Team gave me the thumb's up sign, followed by the good news,' Angela paused 'I just shrieked, and the tears fell down my cheeks.'

Angela's next aim is to appear in the European and World Championships. At the moment she is living with her boyfriend in Guildford, Surrey, and they are planning to marry next year. His name is Mark Richardson, and he is also an athlete. He comes from Maidenhead, and ran the third leg in the 4x400 metres relay at Atlanta, taking a silver medal. They both share the same agent, Martin Watkins, and Angela currently works for an accountancy firm, Tarnel, Kerr and Foster. This was the same company that employed Sally Gunnel until she went to the Barcelona Olympics. Angela is dedicated to training, her coach being Tony Lester, and her employers are satisfied at her working a three day week which of course is of great benefit to her athletic career.

One of Angela Thorp's greatest desires is to win a medal at the Sydney Olympics year 2000. With her outstanding ability, spirit and determination, I think that the Wombwell athlete could well achieve her dream.

10. ARTHUR 'LOCKY'O'LOUGHLIN

Unbeaten World Kick-Box Champion

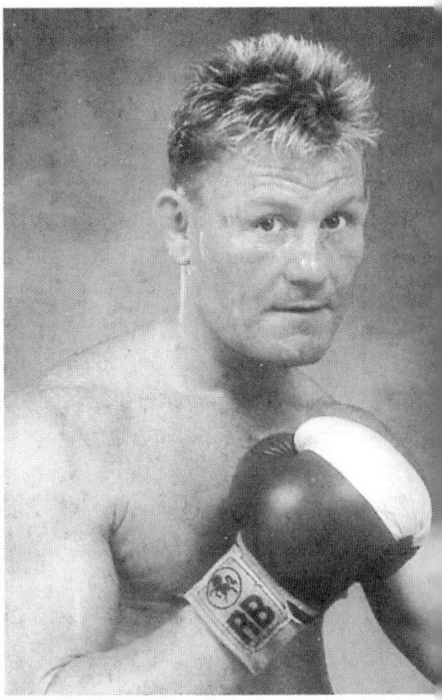

KNOWING that I was on my way to visit the world kick-box champion, Arthur 'Locky' O'Loughlin, made me wonder if there would be any airs and graces about the man. I could not have been more incorrect, he and his wife Christine, made me feel extremely welcome.

Christine, whom he married on 19 October 1974, poured everyone tea, and I began. One of the first things you notice about Arthur O'Loughlin is his enthusiasm. He has a great love of life, and both he and his wife (who takes aerobic classes) are very fit. Arthur was born at 7 Manor Way, Hoyland, on 15 May 1952. In fact, I interviewed him on his forty-fourth birthday. He was the son of Arthur and Minnie, his mother's maiden name being Steele. His late father was Irish, and came over to England to work at out-cropping coal.

Arthur went to school at St Helens, Hoyland, and then to Pope Pius Roman Catholic School, Wath-upon- Dearne. Whilst at these schools he was very sport-orientated, in fact he thought that he would finish up as a footballer in those early days. He was so fond of fighting though, that in the end he settled for karate. His first instructor was Kenny Sykes, at a Church Hall in Darton, and later with Edgar Auckland at the Dorothy Hyman Stadium. This was from 1969 to 1978.

In 1976 Arthur became the South Yorkshire Junior Champion, and then in 1978 he fought David Hoy at the Elizabethan Hall in Manchester, to become the British Lightweight Full Contact Karate Champion. In May, 1979 he received a Black belt from Edgar Auckland, the chief examiner.

I asked Arthur about his ordinary working life whilst he was achieving his ambition in karate. His first job was as a miner at Elsecar Main Colliery, his second was at Parramore's foundry, also at Sheffield, where he was a grinder, then on to market trading in the Barnsley area. In 1984 he took over a Health Studio in the basement of Wombwell Working Men's Club, originally started by Steve Jenkinson. However, before the culmination of Arthur's business, in June 1979, he fought to take the British Full Contact Karate

Welterweight from Gunter Roomes of London, at *The Londoner,* Monk Bretton. Gunter won by one point. In the mid-1980s, Arthur turned professional and carried on with his studio and competition fighting until 1987, when he retired. He and Christine have two daughters, Vicky and Zoe, the former gaining a Black belt at the age of eleven years.

I asked Arthur if everything had gone smoothly throughout his career. Apparently not. Once in the early eighties, when he was going to fight ten rounds of a non-title fight in Indianapolis, his Greek manager based in London, let him down. After feeding Arthur a giant-sized pizza, he told him that he could not accompany him there. Arthur finally set off with just single fare to first New York, then Buffalo, before finally arriving at his destination. He was met and taken to a Butlin style complex. The following morning, Arthur ran seven miles in the searing heat and got lost. Finding his way back, and running all the mileage again, lost him about half a stone in weight. He went to bed and then fought the match. He thought he had won, but the Americans didn't want to award to him, against their three times world champion. The next morning, after a big party which he didn't attend, poor old Arthur had to go knocking on door after door for his money to go home with. Everyone was bleary-eyed and looking at him quite strangely. It took him a long time to find the promoter, the man who owed him his fee. An experience not

Arthur in action in 1984 against Mississippi Champion Jimmy Bland at Atlanta.

Some of the pupils from Arthur's Kick Boxing classes in fighting pose.

to be repeated.

Another time that Arthur could recall in those early days was when he had to travel to Miami in Florida. It was so hot there that people were dying if they didn't have air-conditioning. Arthur set off from England in a three piece mohair suit. He alighted from the plane in a sweltering heat, everyone else was dressed in shorts and skimpy clothing. He was met, and taken from the airport squashed in the back of a limo between two other men. The journey stretched for 90 miles. Arthur thought he was going to die that afternoon, there was so much perspiration pouring off him.

In 1989 Arthur came out of retirement to take on Terry 'Bang Bang' Begue. This time it was on 'home ground', at Aston Villa, Birmingham. His opponent was again from America, and the contest was for the World Kick-Boxing Middleweight title. The bout lasted for twelve gruelling rounds, and Arthur won on a majority decision in front of a crowd of two thousand. He accomplished this magnificent feat by including in his strict diet a glass of Guinness every day, three shredded wheat, and Barnsley Chops!

Arthur has defended his title three times since, and retired unbeaten. He has started his own style of karate, the British Academy of Contact Karate, (B.A.C.K.). He is the founder and has formed his own syllabus. The gradings start with beginner, red belt, yellow, orange, green, and the black. He is also a member of the governing body of karate for all England, Scotland, Ireland and Wales. However, this does not cover kick-boxing.

In September 1989 a surprise party was held for Arthur at the *Horseshoe* pub in Wombwell. To his astonishment, Kenny Sykes came to see him. Arthur must have thought he had seen a ghost, because years earlier, he had seen his old friend's obituary in the paper. Kenny had been seriously ill and someone must have got the wrong end of the stick.

Recovering from the shock, Arthur was over the moon at seeing him. As he remembered, 'It was a very emotional moment, because Ken was the man who made it all possible. If he had not introduced me to karate, I would never have become kick-box world champion'.

I asked Arthur if he had any further ambition. He replied that he wanted to send thirty of his students to take part in the Battle of Atlanta in 1997, the biggest karate event in the world, and for himself to take part in the 'Gladiators' competitions.

The Bodytone Studio raises money for many charitable events. Cheques have been handed over to many worthwhile causes, hospitals and suchlike. Arthur is very dedicated to teaching his students. He has watched them change from scared little children into strong, independent men. He has been billed as 'a local hero with a heart of gold, and hands of steel'. He has great strength and tenacity. When his entrance anthem is played, then all his fans agree that it really befits him, Tina Turner's *Simply The Best.*

Taken at Heathrow airport, a team of 25 fighters from the British Academy of Contact Karate Association, at Bodytone Health Studio.

11. MEMORIES OF REGINALD LAYBOURN

Old-time Boxer and Trainer

REG LAYBOURN has been around for quite a while. If anyone needs to know about boxing in the Barnsley district, this is the man to see. Reg was born on 27 November 1905, to parents Frederick and Emma. He was raised in the Monk Bretton area, and went to the local school. Unfortunately, being small of stature, he became the victim of bullies at a tender age. Reg did not want to go through life unable to defend himself, so when he left school and went to work as a miner, he took himself off to train with Charlie Glover, first at a gym based at the *Royal Oak*, and then at the *Lord Nelson Hotel*, classed at the time as the finest gym in England. It was there that Reg learned the art of fisticuffs.

The first important bout for Reg was at the *Theatre Royal*, Wellington Street. Reg reminisced, 'The date was 11 June 1926, it was during the miners' strike and money was hard to come by'. A variety show had arrived at the theatre, along with two professional boxers, Dick Manning and Jos Keogh. The manager challenged the audience for someone to fight either of the two men. Reg took him up and put his name down to fight Keogh but the manager changed it to Manning, the heavier and more experienced of the two. The bout went the distance, six rounds, and Reg lost on points, but it was a thrilling experience for him, particularly so when he was presented with the purse of £4, a lot of money in those days. The year following, he travelled to Newcastle to fight, and won £3-10 shillings (3.50p). Over the next thirteen years, he fought professionally as a fly-weight, about seventy times, weighing-in around 7stone 2lbs. He was still working as a miner, so it formed a good

THEATRE ROYAL
BARNSLEY.
Week Commencing Monday, June 7, 1926, for Six Nights
6-50 - TWICE NIGHTLY - 9.
A CHALLENGE!
In submitting his new Revue "ALLSPICE" for the first time in Yorkshire, Mr. Geo. Sax is presenting the Famous 7-stone Boxers—
DICK MANNING
AND
JOS KEOGH
WHO ARE BOTH CHAMPIONS IN THEIR CLASS
Mr. Sax, in conjunction with the Theatre Management, is offering a handsome sum of money to anyone at the above weight who can stand up to either of the above boxers for Six Rounds.
Both Manning and Keogh will box Three Rounds at each performance, and Competitors are asked to hand in their names to the Theatre Management, who will arrange for the contests to take place.
YOU MUST SEE
"ALLSPICE"
A Galaxy of Gayness and Girls in 20 Scenes.
Get the Theatre Habit.
'Phone 103

Reg's first fight was with Dick Manning. He lost on points.

supplement to his wages. Unfortunately, he broke his hand when he was fighting at a match in Barnsley His opponent was a man named 'Young' Ahern. 'Ironically', Reg said, 'I had won ten matches straight off before this bout and was in great shape'.

The injury threw Reg out of work for the next sixteen weeks causing much hardship for him due to lack of money. This decided him to travel along another avenue, still in the boxing world, but as trainer, boxer, masseur, second, anything that he was called upon to do. He started his own gymnasium at the *Blackamoor Hotel*, Barnsley, now demolished. In later years, he was to take over Charlie Glover's gym at the *Junction Inn*. Stephen and Graham Laybourn two of Reg's three sons, now take care of it. I asked Reg if they used boxing gloves in his early days, or if it was bare-knuckle fighting. He told me that he had always used gloves, but the Boxing Board of Control didn't exist until 1929, so it was pretty varied until then. Reg travelled around the country to venues but it was hard work because he still had his work as a miner, plus he had to go to the gym a lot for training practice. One of the most popular boxing rings in Barnsley

Going at it hammer and tongs. Jackie Swann (Barnsley) versus Tiny Smith (Sheffield) at the Dillington Park Stadium, 24 July 1926.

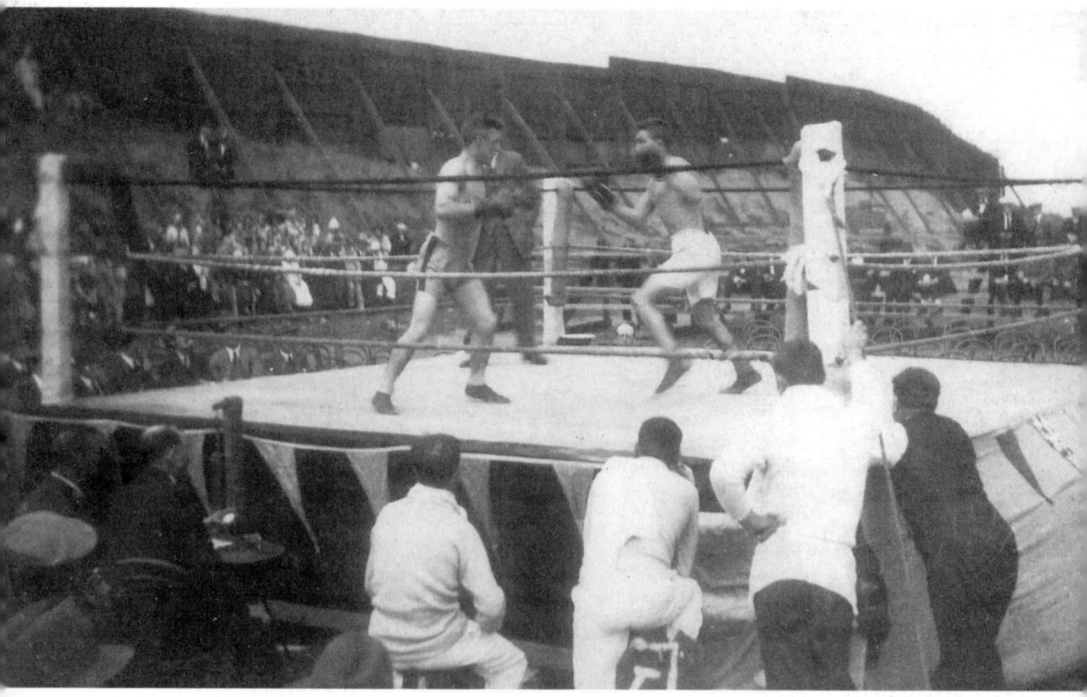

Fast and furious, Jim Birch in challenging pose.

A superbly fit Charles Hardcastle taken in his heyday.

Jackie Swann, dynamite comes in small bundles.

Dick Roughly, a fine figure of a man.

was the Stadium at Midland Road. 'Here,' Reg said, 'you could see boxers such as Chuck Parker, Billy Jones, Jim Birch, Matt Moran and numerous others.

Another 'good un' in Reg's eyes was Jackie Swann. He weighed 7st 12lbs and could hand out very severe punishment. One of his events was held before an audience of 20,000 at the Moor, Sheffield. This bout was for a £50 side-stake against Tiny Smith, known as the Sheffield Terror. He couldn't terrorise the Barnsley fly-weight though, who won the match on points and brought his opponent into submission with a great left-hand throughout. Jackie had a brother Billy who was also a boxer and fought under the name of Billy Brown.

In an article written by Ben Green, in the *Green'Un*, 1956, he mentions the exploits of another Barnsley boxer:

> *A grand nine stone boy from Barnsley was Jim Birch, who also carved out for himself a formidable record. On one of our Leeds charity shows he was billed against Young Johnny Brown (London), who came with a big reputation. It was all over inside a round. Birch connected with a vicious right-hook and Brown was down for the full count. In 1929, Jim beat Len (Tiger) Smith of Birmingham, in Belfast. They met again in Leeds and Smith turned the tables, winning a great contest on points. Also in 1929, Birch beat Ernie Bicknole, Jim McQuade (Scotland), Alf Howard (Liverpool), and George Lawson (Hull), on points. He also defeated Jack Glover at Barnsley for a side-stake and purse. All these contests were fifteen-rounders. One of his bouts that I have good reason to recall was that against Jack Casey in December 1928, on the programme for the dependents of the late Dick Roughly. In the seventh round, Jim hit the 'Sunderland assassin' with such terrible force on that so-called cast-iron jaw of his, that he took a count and then, struggling to his feet, floundered all over the ring on legs that were like jelly. I had to stop the fight in Birch's favour in the seventh round.*

At this point Reg flourished a photograph of Jimmy Birch. His wife Doris and I remarked that he had been a good-looking man. 'Aye,' Reg laughed, 'until he got some hammer.' Looking through Reg's memorabilia, I came across a reference to Charlie Hardcastle, who in Reg's words was another 'belter' from Barnsley. A man who took the British feather-weight crown with a first round knock-out! The *Barnsley Chronicle* published a report of this match, against Alf Wye of London, held at the National Sporting Club on 4 June 1917:

> *For some time, Hardcastle's form has been of the in-and-out variety, a circumstance due to the fact that he is engaged in coal*

mining, and he has frequently had to take the ring practically untrained. For Monday's contest he had quite a good preparation at Whetstone, and took the arena looking very fit. Wye, among other things, has twice beaten Bob Cotton (who defeated Hardcastle) and disposed of Curly Walker. At the weigh-in, Wye drew 8st 13lbs, and Hardcastle was a quarter of a pound more. Wye was favourite.

The bout proved a great disappointment. The men entered the ring shortly before 11 o'clock, and less time than usual was taken up with preliminaries. Wye tried to cut out the work, but Hardcastle met him well, and the pair were going at a fast rate when the Barnsley man caught his rival with a left-hook to the jaw. Down went Wye as though shot, and he was unable to rise before ten seconds expired. Hardcastle thus won the bout almost before one could realise it had started. The Sportsman described it as one of the speediest victories

Barnsley pugilists of the past. (names unknown)

on record. Charlie in fact was the only winner of the Lonsdale Belt who never even touched it, or set eyes on it during the whole time he was supposed to be holding it. Welshman Llew Edwards was the previous holder of the belt. He had won it on 31 May 1915, when he met Owen Moran of Birmingham, the latter being disqualified in the tenth round.

Managed by George Bailleu, Edwards went to Australia and had the belt on show everywhere he fought. He was called upon to defend the belt and consequently relinquished it. But it took him a long time to get it off to England. When the manager of the National Sporting Club, 'Peggy' Bettinson matched Hardcastle and Billy Fanner of Wales, in a title eliminator on 23 April 1917, he was sure the belt was on it's way. Charlie disposed of Fanner in the seventh round and was matched with Alf Wye for the vacant title on 17 June 1917. By that time it was expected that the belt would have arrived from Australia.

Reg remarked at this point, that it was a darned shame that Charlie had never held the belt, because on 5 November 1917, he lost the title to Tancy Lee at the NSC. It was handed over, and poor old Charlie, or 'Toddy' as he was affectionately known by, never even saw the belt. He was born in Thomas Street, Worsbrough Bridge, and died at the age of 66 at his home in Taylor Row, Sheffield Road in 1960.

Reg as he is today at the sprightly age of 91.

I asked Reg if he had helped to train anyone who had done particularly well. He pondered for a while, 'I've had lots of good blokes. Billy Calvert, he went for the British title but lost on points to the champion, Howard Winston. I also had a chap come to ask me to take his son on, he too achieved fame. The youngster's name was Shaun Doyle, he's doing very well you know, got his own business, but he's still t'same lad.'

I could tell by the warmth in Reg's tone of voice that he still has a soft spot for his 'lads', even though most of them are gone. He said that times were hard in his day, but he'd enjoyed his career. Reg still gets enthusiastic when he talks about the old days, and who can blame him, he has led a most interesting life.

12. TERRY HALPIN

Boxer and National Coal Board Champion

TERRY HALPIN, boxing champion was born at 71 Elliott Terrace, New Scarborough, Wombwell in 1941. His parents, Mary and Chris, had four other children: Jack, Chris, Bill and sister Irene. School-days were spent at St Michael's, Low Valley. Terry first became interested in boxing at a very young age. His father, Chris Halpin, was the manager of a coal mine in Malaya and he brought home to England a pair of boxing gloves as a present for Terry. This fired the young lad with ambition, and at eleven years old he went training at *The Bull's Head*, a pub at Brampton. The Boxing Club was in an upstairs room. Terry won his first fight with a youngster named Lowther at Sheffield. Although this was early days, it gave him the desire to carry on. A man from Brampton, Michael Lyons, encouraged him throughout this period.

On leaving school at fifteen, Terry's first job was at Qualter Smith's, the iron foundry in Barnsley. He thought of going down the mine because at that time boxing as a sport was a big event for the NCB and anyone who showed ability was greatly encouraged. Coalfields throughout the country entered their own contenders for their area, amidst fierce competition. Terry achieved his ambition to work down a mine and started at Darfield Main Colliery when he was sixteen. He took advantage of the training facilities at Darfield and Mitchell gymnasium and entered NCB boxing matches. Initially his trainer was a man named Billy McHale. Technically, Terry admitted, he should not have been able to enter matches until

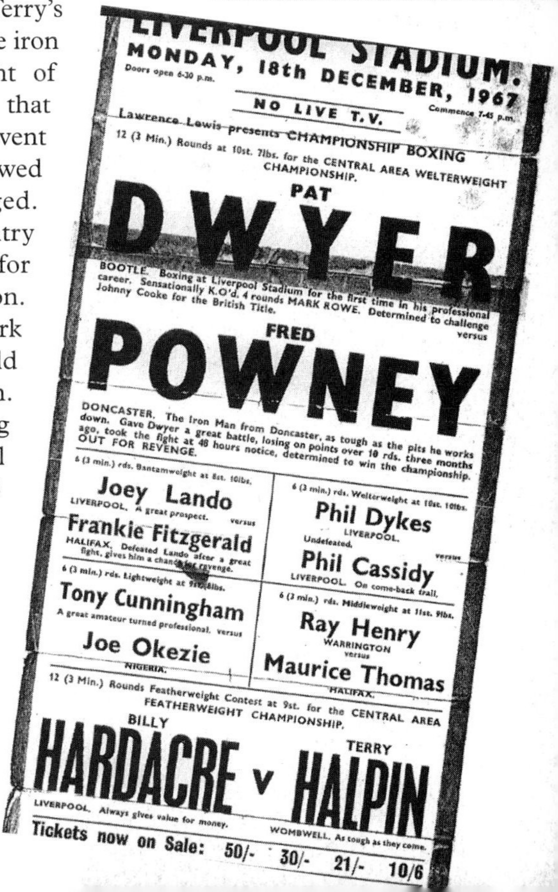

LIVERPOOL STADIUM.
MONDAY, 18th DECEMBER, 1967
Doors open 6-30 p.m.
NO LIVE T.V.
Commence 7-45 p.m.
Lawrence Lewis presents CHAMPIONSHIP BOXING
12 (3 Min.) Rounds at 10st. 7lbs. for the CENTRAL AREA WELTERWEIGHT CHAMPIONSHIP.
PAT
DWYER
BOOTLE. Boxing at Liverpool Stadium for the first time in his professional career. Sensationally K.O'd. 4 rounds MARK ROWE. Determined to challenge Johnny Cooke for the British Title.
versus
FRED
POWNEY
DONCASTER. The Iron Man from Doncaster, as tough as the pits he works down. Gave Dwyer a great battle, losing on points over 10 rds. three months ago, took the fight at 48 hours notice, determined to win the championship. OUT FOR REVENGE.
6 (3 min.) rds. Bantamweight at 8st. 10lbs.
Joey Lando
LIVERPOOL. A great prospect.
versus
Frankie Fitzgerald
HALIFAX. Defeated Lando after a great fight, gives him a chance for revenge.
Tony Cunningham
A great amateur turned professional.
versus
Joe Okezie
NIGERIA.
6 (3 min.) rds. Welterweight at 10st. 10lbs.
Phil Dykes
LIVERPOOL.
Undefeated.
versus
Phil Cassidy
LIVERPOOL. On come-back trail.
6 (3 min.) rds. Middleweight at 11st. 9lbs.
Ray Henry
WARRINGTON
versus
Maurice Thomas
HALIFAX.
12 (3 Min.) Rounds Featherweight Contest at 9st. for the CENTRAL AREA FEATHERWEIGHT CHAMPIONSHIP.
BILLY
HARDACRE v HALPIN
TERRY
LIVERPOOL. Always gives value for money.
WOMBWELL. As tough as they come.
Tickets now on Sale: 50/- 30/- 21/- 10/6

Poster from Liverpool Stadium 1967

In fighting form in his amateur days.

he was seventeen, but in reality he glossed over the truth and fought at sixteen. He was doing two or three fights a day, and quickly worked his way through to the National Finals. He lost, but at only sixteen, it was very good practice for him. Terry mentioned that the manager of the colliery, Mr Jones, was very good to him and helped in any way possible.I asked him about the kind of prizes that he had won in his early years, from aged eleven. He said that he could remember his first, it was a pair of candlesticks. He had also won numerous watches, but one of his most prized possessions which he still has today, is a twenty-one piece tea-set, won in the 1950s. 'It's a beauty,' he remarked. He also added, that Jack Land,who was refereeing at the time, used to let him have his pick of the prizes.

Terry started his fighting career as a bantam-weight, but quickly advanced to feather-weight, which he maintained until retirement. He weighed between 8st 12lbs to 8st 13lbs, and said that he was 'fighting fit' at this weight. As a junior he became the Northern Counties Champion, and an Amateur Boxing Association Finalist in

Terry being presented with the Feather-weight Title Trophy by Lord Robens at Wolverhampton. 1962-63.

1958, fighting at the Royal Albert Hall in London. As a senior, he held the North Eastern Counties Championship from 1959 until 1964. He also held the Northern Counties Championship from 1962 until 1964. Terry's highest achievement though, was the National Coal Board Championship of Great Britain which he held from 1961 to 1964. In fact Terry was the last holder and the trophy now rests in a London museum. He was allowed to keep it throughout his winning years, but when the Championships folded up, he had to hand it back. It was a great honour for Yorkshire that Terry was able to achieve this unique position.

His first opponent for this particular match in 1961 was Ken Brett. Terry won with a knockout, incidentally Ken was the brother of Eric Brett, a professional boxer, and another brother, Eddie, whom Terry had already fought and beaten. 1962 saw him win again with Cyril Thomas, he too had a famous brother, Eddie. The year after he took on Ken Jones from Wales, and then in 1964 came George Shields. A report from Keith Lodge, sports reporter from the *Barnsley Chronicle*, ran as follows:

With the National NCB finals taking place in Barnsley for the first time last Friday, 6 March 1964, it was fitting that the best boxing of the evening should be provided by the one remaining local representative.

This was of course, 22 years-old Terry Halpin, the fitter's mate from Wombwell, who was bidding to win the feather-weight title for the fourth successive year, having already established a record by winning it three years on the trot. Halpin, with former European Police Middle-weight Champion, Brian Sutton in his corner, delighted his home crowd at the packed Civic Hall with a copybook display of boxing to beat twenty-two year old Scotsman George Shields on points. Shields had Halpin worried half-way through the first round when he staggered the Darfield Main boy with a right to the head. For several heart-stopping seconds, Halpin back-pedalled furiously, defending himself only by sheer instinct as Shields crowded in, throwing punches to the head and body, but he weathered the storm and at the end of the round it was he who had the Scot in trouble on the ropes.

Again, as the bell signalled the end of round two, Shields was taking punishment on the ropes and perspiring, face as red as a Barnsley football shirt, looking more than a little perplexed. In the third round it was Halpin all the way. He might have made a mistake by mixing it as much as he did with an opponent who had already hurt him, but he was not caught again. Many of his fans however, would have preferred him to rely more exclusively on his left-hand jab, surely one of the most powerfully devastating and accurate in amateur boxing. This was one bout which went as anticipated.

After this particular win Terry boxed for another two years and at the age of twenty four he turned professional. By this time, he had fought around 350 bouts including a fight with Ken Buchanan, a Scotsman who became World Champion. His manager by now was Ken Richardson from Retford, Nottinghamshire. Also during these latter years he married his wife, Tina, and they had three children, Cheryl, Shaun, and Dawn. He stayed in the boxing game until he was thirty years old. One of his biggest disappointments was to be offered a place in the International Boxing Team, representing England against Russia, and then being dropped at the last moment with no satisfactory explanation from the officials. Terry really enjoyed his boxing days fighting alongside men such as Joe Taylor, Brian Sutton and Frank Walshaw. He also trained with Brian Glover and Shaun Doyle at the *Junction Inn*, Doncaster Road, Barnsley.

Terry today with some trophies.

A lot of Terry's most memorable professional matches were held at the National Sporting Club in London. For example: 5 July 1965, he fought Jimmy Anderson, a feather-weight who later became the British Champion; 29 June 1965 he fought Ali Juma; 23 May 1966, Bobby Davis; 21 November 1966 Monty Loud; 29 November 1966, Colin Lake; 6 February 1967, Hugh Baxter; and 22 April 1968, Joey Lando. In all, Terry fought around 50 bouts as a professional.

These days, Terry keeps fit by working as a scaffolder on building sites. He still has that wiry look that has come from keeping himself in tip-top condition. Terry and Tina went their separate ways many years ago, and his wife, Lillian, has been by his side for the last twenty years. She has two grown-up children, Damon and Emily.

The great National Coal Board Championship Trophy days are over now. Terry was part of that life in the 1950/60s and looks back at his sporting achievements with pride.

13. CHRISTOPHER SAUNDERS

Welter-Weight Boxer

CHRIS SAUNDERS, a young Barnsley boxer is climbing the ladder of success. Born 15 August 1969, to parents Barry and Janet, he has lived in the Hoyland area all his life. His mum died of cancer when Chris was aged twelve, so sadly she has not been around to see his achievements. His father Barry, who did some boxing himself when young has been a source of encouragement. Chris's grandfather succeeded in becoming an Army Boxing champion. Chris went to Hoyland Common Junior School and then on to Kirk Balk Comprehensive. It was here that he first became interested in boxing. His father took him along to see Arthur O'Loughlin at his gym in Wombwell for some training.

By the age of sixteen and still at school, Chris had fought about 50 to 60 amateur fights, working his way through to the quarter-finals of the National Association of Boys Clubs' Northern East Counties Championships. After leaving school Chris worked on the YTS scheme for two years at a Stocksbridge Steelworks. He then did furniture delivery for a year followed by forklift truck driving at a food warehouse. Leaving Arthur's, he trained for a short while at the gym at the *Black Bull* at Stairfoot and also Wombwell Baths, the trainer being Derek Walker. Chris then went under the management of Frank Maloney, based at the Henry Cooper Gym, Old Kent Road, London. It was here in 1990 that Chris turned professional. This was the same stable that had Lennox-Lewis on it's books, the former heavy-weight world champion. After Maloney, Chris transferred to Ken Richardson of Retford, Nottingham for a short time. However, in 1993, wanting to further his career, he travelled to Wincobank, Sheffield and now trains under the watchful eye of Brendan Ingle who also manages Naseem Hamed, another world class boxer.

When Chris was 21 he fought as a light welter-weight at 10 stone, he gradually put another half-stone on and now fights as a welter-weight. He has had around thirty professional fights, as Chris put it, 'I am now fighting the best guys in the business.' At the age of 26 and on 15 September 1995, he got a crack at the British Welter-weight title against Del Bryan at Mansfield. It was an exciting fight and Chris won on points over twelve memorable rounds. A summary of the match was given in the *Barnsley Chronicle* by Keith Lodge:

FIRST ROUND. A sensational start as Saunders lands a stunning cross to the side of the jaw to dump Bryan on to the seat of his pants midway through the round just when the champion seemed to be gaining early control. Saunder's round. 10-9

SECOND ROUND. Bryan appears to have completely recovered from the knock-down. His superior boxing skills give him the edge and he lands some good punches. Bryan takes it. 10-9

THIRD ROUND. Saunders launches a tremendous assault and has Bryan in trouble, but he sustains a cut eye in the process. Another cut opens up around the other eye and blood is pouring down both cheeks at the end of the round. Bryan shades it. 10-9

FOURTH ROUND. Ernie Fossey does a remarkable job on the cuts to stop the bleeding, but Bryan's southpaw jab is beginning to dictate the pattern of the fight and he begins to pick up the points. However, Saunders staggers the favourite again near the end of the round and Bryan is pleased to hear the bell. Bryan's round. 10-9

FIFTH ROUND. The same story. Jab, jab, jab from Bryan, Saunders struggling to find a way past it. The Hoyland fighter is being heavily out-scored at this stage and is falling well behind. It may need a knock-out to win it. Bryan. 10-9

Friendly sparring with World class boxing champion Prince Naseem Hamed.

SIXTH ROUND. Bryan still in control in the first half of the round, but then Saunders catches him again and launches a fierce two-fisted attack towards the end of the round to give him a share of the points. 10-10

SEVENTH ROUND. Great pressure from Saunders. Bryan begins to look ragged. Another big right hand rocks the champion. By far the best round for the challenger, who wins it. 10-9

EIGHTH ROUND. The decisive three minutes. As Saunders' right puts Bryan down for the second time and he looks stunned. Saunders charges in with a tremendous flurry of punches and pins Bryan on the ropes. Lefts and rights rain in, but Bryan holds on and survives. A big round for Saunders. 10-9

NINTH ROUND. Saunders on top for the first half of the round, but Bryan seems to get his second wind and begins to get his act together. His jab comes into play again and he lands some very useful punches. Even round. 10-10

TENTH ROUND. Bryan takes the fight to Saunders, who begins to look a little weary. The champion appears to have recovered his composure, but is still susceptible to a clubbing right hand from Saunders. Bryan's round. 10-9

ELEVENTH ROUND. Saunders lands that right again and Bryan is forced to hold on. Then it is Saunders turn to hold as he takes half a dozen punches without reply. Right at the end of the round the Hoyland lad catches Bryan off balance and the champion reels to the canvas only to be saved by the bell. That knock-down swung the round in Saunder's favour. 10-9

TWELFTH ROUND. It looks like it could be all on this round, and Saunders makes sure of the verdict by flooring Bryan for the fourth time in the fight with a superb uppercut. Saunders' round, 10-9, and Saunders' title by the narrowest of margins, 117-117.

The Lonsdale Belt was his, but this happy state of affairs was not to last for very long however because about three months later he lost it again to Kevin Leushing from London. In retrospect, the circumstances of the fight were not very good. Chris had fought Leushing and defeated him in the past so he was very hopeful that events would work out more successfully than they actually did. The day before the match was due, Chris travelled to London, on 9 September 1996. He was in a van with about seven others when a bomb went off in Canary Wharf. They were about one hundred yards from the blast, but the whole van shook and the occupants were showered with glass. It was very unnerving, the match was cancelled and Chris was sent back to Barnsley. He had to travel back on 12

September, a couple of days later to try again. Unfortunately, the fight was stopped in the third round, the honours going to his opponent. 'In my opinion,' Barry said, 'The fight should not have taken place for at least two weeks, in order for everything to settle down.' I said to Chris that it must have been nerve-wracking. Chris grinned, 'Even Mike Tyson gets nervous before a fight.' He added, 'Anyway, I haven't given up, I shall try to get it back.'

Chris has fought abroad twice, once with Germany's former European champion, Jose Ferrera. This man had fought 32 professional fights, losing one. He'd knocked 30 people out. Chris Saunders knocked him out in the second round, a great achievement. The second fight abroad, December 1994, was with Roberto Wellin from Sweden. He was the former European Amateur Boxing champion who had been trained and managed by Angelo Dundee who coached the great Muhammed Ali. Chris knocked Wellin out in the eighth-round.

Chris has two sisters, Leslie, who unfortunately has spina bifida, and Linda (Mrs DuPront) who lives in France. Linda is well known in Chantilly, the area in which she lives because of her career as a jockey. Chris is making great strides in the boxing game, he's fighting fit, and has a very good future in front of him.

Chris proudly holding the Lonsdale Belt

14. SHAUN DOYLE

Boxer and Central Area Champion

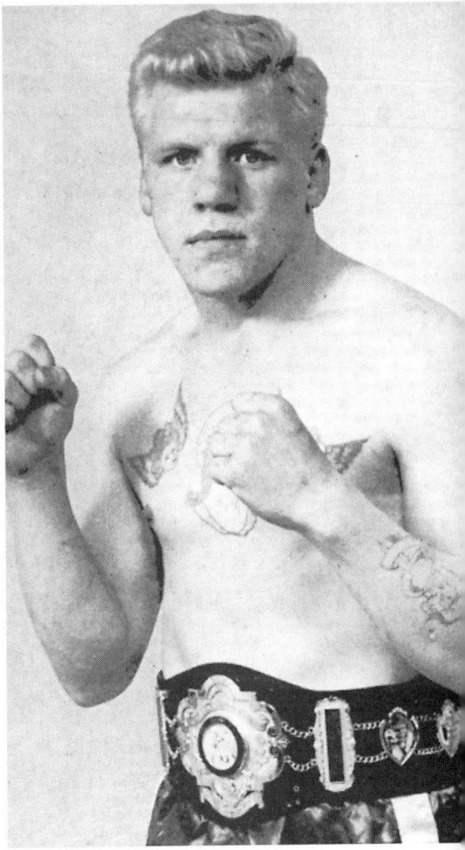

I MET SHAUN DOYLE, his wife Irene, and their son Grant at the family home in Dodworth. I was introduced to them by my cousin, Ken Brown, and his wife Margaret, who is the sister of Irene. Ken had already assured me that Shaun was a very down-to-earth bloke and this turned out to be true. I was given a very warm welcome. The trappings of success are enjoyed, but taken very much in their stride.

Shaun began by giving me a little bit of his background. He was born on 1 January 1945, at Union Court, off Union Street, Barnsley. He added, 'We lived at the back of where *The Old Warrior* pub used to be.' His parents were Joseph and Elsie, and Shaun was raised along with his brothers Joseph and Peter, and sisters, Elsie, Annie, and Mary. The children went to Holy Rood School. Throughout Shaun's schooldays, he was very much into sporting activities, besides boxing he also enjoyed football, playing in later years for Wyn Street United. At the age of fifteen, Shaun started his working life down the mine at North Gawber Colliery. His father encouraged him to box and at the age of sixteen Shaun began in earnest. He was training at the gym at the back of the *Junction Inn,* and there he met Jim Birch, an old-time boxer, and Charlie Glover, the father of Brian Glover, wrestler and actor. Both the men spotted the potential in Shaun and as he put it, 'They helped to push me forward.' He was also greatly influenced by Reg Laybourn, another old-time boxer and masseur for Barnsley Football Club. Shaun had a total of five amateur fights before turning professional. His last amateur fight was with a kid called Jackie Turpin, at Leeds Town Hall. Shaun knocked the NCB contender down and out in the first round whereupon the referee stopped the fight. He disqualified Shaun for allegedly hitting with an open glove. Shaun said that a great future had been forecast for his opponent, and he himself was just an outsider coming into the game. The decision of the referee in this match helped to decide Shaun into turning professional.

Shaun's first match in the world of the professional, fighting as a welter-weight at 10st 7lbs, was against Tommy Waterworth, the Welsh Champion. Tommy had just come back from boxing in the Olympics, but Shaun knocked him out in the first round at Liverpool Stadium. His next opponent was the Irish Champion, Des Ray, whom he beat on points at Sheffield City Hall. Andy Wiper, the Scottish Champion came next in London at the National Sporting Club. He too was beaten.

Shaun's trainer at this moment in time was an ex-boxer called Peter Bates. He used to be a heavy-weight and lived in Chesterfield. His most noted fight was with Henry Cooper, whom he beat in the third round. Shaun added that boxers were not cosseted and transported around in those days like they are now with an entourage. 'No', Shaun smiled, 'I had to pack my little bag with my gum-shield etc, and trot off under my own steam.'

Shaun fought his way up the ladder in order to gain the coveted Central Area Championship Belt. Contenders for the three years that Shaun had it were Fred Powney and Gordon McTeer, who challenged him twice. Shaun was allowed to keep the nine-carat gold belt permanently after his third challenge fight. The next title on the menu was hopefully, British Welter-Weight Champion. This tilt at the title resulted in one of the most gruelling matches that Shaun had fought up till then. His opponent was Johnny Cooke, the British Champion. The match took place at Liverpool Stadium 6 May 1967. Shaun said that the place was packed to the rafters, and the atmosphere was electric. It was a bitter disappointment when Shaun suffered defeat with a narrow points decision. The fight lasted for fifteen blood-spattered rounds. Keith Lodge, *Barnsley Chronicle* sports reporter, summed up the feeling of the people in our area:

> *Barnsley can be proud of Shaun Doyle. He put up a tremendous fight against a vastly more experienced opponent, showing a mixture of typical bull-dog Yorkshire determination and the fighting spirit which belies his Irish ancestry.*
>
> *Ironically, however, it could well be that this self-same courage and eagerness to 'mix-it' cost him the Londsdale Belt. Obviously obeying instructions, he threw caution to the winds with furious two-fisted attacks on Cooke's body in the early rounds, with the intention of wearing the older man down. Yet amazingly, in the eleventh round,*

> *Shaun, the pupil, mastered the master at his own game. He almost jabbed Cooke's head off with a series of uncannily accurate lefts and he proceeded to pick up points with a beautiful display of long-range boxing skills.*

Heavy-weight, Johnny Prescott, who had been training with Shaun, remarked, 'Shaun lad, you may not have won, but you've really done Yorkshire proud.'

Shaun as he is today, enjoying the fruits of his labour.

Al Phillips, who was Shaun's manager, commented, 'I was proud of the way Shaun fought. He surprised a lot of people and I know that when he gets another chance, he will win the title.'

This was not to be however, Shaun, who had received his professional licence at eighteen, decided to retire from boxing at twenty three. He had fought 26 times, losing 3 and drawing 2. He reversed two of his losses, but the third was the fight with Johnny Cooke which was never returned. A pity really, because Shaun may have come out on top the second time, with the knowledge that he had gained from the first match.

In a turnaround of careers, he and Irene became landlord and landlady of the *Plough*, Doncaster Road, Barnsley, now demolished. I asked Shaun what were his thoughts on running a pub. He declared with a grin, that there were better fights in there than in the ring. After five years, in 1973, they left the pub and Shaun invested in a car-pitch at Worsbrough Dale. Ten years after in 1983, he started a security business in Barnsley. He decided that there was a lot of potential around, because as Shaun described it, 'Things were getting a bit harum-scarum.' It was a wise move, because his business never looked back. He hired doormen, bodyguards, and persons to transport payrolls etc. His son Grant, looks after the Static Guard Security side of the business now.

Irene and Shaun had another son named Dean, who was killed in a motor-bike accident when he was fifteen. This was a shattering blow to the family, and Shaun who had become a Catholic, turned to his faith again to try and help him through his grief. This in turn has led to Shaun giving help and support to disabled children in the Barnsley area, financially and otherwise, and accompanying them on trips to Lourdes in France.

Shaun helps to train youngsters to box in his spare time these days. He also takes his two dogs for long walks, a good way for him to keep fit. My cousin Ken had already said to me, (with a grin I might add) 'Annie, those dogs are as soft as butter, you could stroke them all day,' adding, 'once you get to know them!' Well I looked at the two Rottweilers as they were being ushered away, (they had lovely toothpaste white teeth) and decided to pass on that one.

If I were to describe Shaun Doyle, I would say that he is a man in complete charge of his life. He has good business acumen which shows in the huge Security Empire that he has built, but I would also say that he is a humanist with a great generosity of spirit. It was an afternoon to remember at Irene and Shaun's home, lots of laughs with them, Ken and Margaret, myself and husband Clive.

15. ENA FRETWELL

Memories of Barnsley's Sporting Past

ENA FRETWELL, born 6 April 1913, and now living at Worsbrough is an old and valued friend of mine. She has many memories of Barnsley's sporting past which rather surprised me, because until I started to research this book our conversations had centred around subjects other than sport. Ena's maiden name was Berry, and she and her sister Ida, and brothers Charlie and Ernest, resided with their parents Harriet and Charles William Berry at 54 Waltham Street, Barnsley. Ena said that her brother Ernest, 'Tucker' as he was known by, was a very keen sportsman, indulging in boxing, darts and football, playing centre-forward for Worsbrough Common at Dillington in the 1920s/30s.

Ena told me the story which led up to her living next door to an old Barnsley boxer, 'Chuck' Parker. When she was seven, she was orphaned, her father died aged 52, followed by the death of her mother at 49. Her elder sister Ida, who was 24, helped bring Ena up until she left school at 13 and was then sent to relations at Leicester to work in the mills. This lasted until she was 17 and then Ena became homesick for her family and came back to Barnsley. Meanwhile, her married sister was living at 4 Back Waltham Street, next to the Parkers at number 2.

'I thought the world of Chuck's mother', Ena said, 'she treated me like a daughter. When her son was fighting and it was being broadcast on the wireless, she would be hunched over the set saying, 'Hush Ena'. If he won, she would jump up in the air, kissing and hugging her. Ena used to mix Chuck a drink of eggs and sherry in the morning after he had come in from his morning run. She was also a good cook and in return for Mrs Parker's kindness to her would often do the family baking. Chuck loved her egg, bacon and cheese pies. He married Elizabeth, 'Tizzy' Beevers, and they went to live at the end of the street with a family named Oldfields. Ena added that it was a row of only five houses, so everybody knew each other. Indeed, it was there that Ena met her husband, George Fretwell. He had gone to lodge with Mrs Parker, and after their courtship they married in 1932, when Ena was 19. Taking lodgers in was common practice in those days Ena said because times were very hard.

I asked Ena why Charlie Parker had been given his nickname. 'Oh that's easy,' she replied, 'his sister married another Charles, so the boxer was named Chuck, to differentiate.' Ena has kept a cutting from a newspaper article written many years ago by a Mr Ronnie

'Chuck' Parker in his fighting da

Ena in 1996 reflecting on boxer
of the past.

An amicable gathering of men taken in old Waltham Street; From left to right:
Back row
Unknown, Unknown, Archie Hirst, Jimmy Oldfield, 'Chuck' Parker, 'Tucker' Berry, Unknown.
Front row
Unknown, Wilf Slater, Unknown, Mick Barker, Unknown, 'Tue' Barker, Tom Jones.

Right: **Billy Jones' fighting stance, (Chuck's deadly rival).**

Opposite left:
A line-up of Barnsley's grand old boxers; From left to right:
Charlie Parker, Jim Birch, Charlie Glover, Harold Huxley, Charlie Hardcastle, Norman Ratford, Tommy Winder, Fred Holding.

Wharton, here are a few extracts:

Barnsley has the distinction of producing one British champion when Charlie Hardcastle won the feather-weight title during the First World War. During the 1930's the coalmining centre came near to proclaiming a second when the town's own Chuck Parker challenged for the welter-weight title. Young Chuck was only six when Hardcastle became champion and put Barnsley on the boxing map. He first donned boxing gloves during the idle periods at his job in the mining industry. Encouraged by the sparring displays with his workmates, the next stage was to commence gymnasium work at Fred Holden's gym off Sheffield Road.

Holden's gym, which was later run by Bill Birch, was the training centre for Barnsley's foremost ring exponents. Billy Jones, Jim Birch, Jack Skelly, that good bantam from Cudworth Bob Watson, and the likeable Matt Moran, were all regulars, and even Hardcastle himself, though retired, popped in to give advice. Nine months after his first gym work Chuck at 16, made his debut at the Drill Hall in Barnsley, his opponent being another local, Frank Marshall. Only days before his first fight Chuck hurt his right hand. Nothing was going to stop him appearing in the ring, and although the injury was the main reason for his defeat, Chuck wasn't dispirited, his handicap had made him use his left hand more and was good experience for the apprentice. A week or two later, he out-pointed Marshall at the same venue.

Ronnie Wharton went on to list some of Chuck Parker's next fights. These were against Curly Williams at Normanton, Manchester's Jack Hudson and Jim Learoyd, the Northern area champion from Leeds, the latter two being held at Preston. The write-up continues:

In the same Barnsley backstreets as Chuck, lived Billy Jones, Barnsley's Northern area light-weight champion. Jones, the elder by five years, had won the honour of being the town's top boxer and Chuck's rapid rise over the last few months had started to threaten his position. Deadly rivals in the late 1920s and early 1930s and good friends today it was only natural that the two men should meet in the ring. The meeting was at Dearne Football Ground one Monday, Jones proving much too clever for the youngster and too experienced, and he gained a points victory. After 20 or 30 more fights in which he won most, Chuck made another challenge to Jones, so keen was he for a return. He was still managing his own affairs and would have fought for nothing to have the chance of beating his rival.

The rivalry had made the fight a grudge match and so keen were fight fans that Barnsley Stadium (where the bus station now stands) was packed. The fight captured Barnsley's imagination and money changed hands like nobody's business as the townsfolk betted on their individual hero. Unfortunately the affair, much to the crowds disappointment, only went one round. Chuck was disqualified at the end of the round for alleged hitting after the bell.

Mr Wharton carried on by listing some more of Chuck's important fights. He fought Sheffield light-weight champion Johnny Cuthbert, (with whom he became close friends), Harry Corbett, former feather-weight champion, Jim Learoyd again (a victory this time), Vic Meadsley of Preston, Jack Lord of Bolton, Leo Phillips, Carl Barton and Don Jones, the Welsh light-weight champion whom he knocked out in four rounds. In the Midlands he knocked out Peter Nolan of Walsall, beat Jack Moody the Welsh welter-weight champion in nine rounds and had a points victory over Freddie Dyer at Smethwick. Many matches followed involving Chuck travelling to Scotland, Brighton, London and elsewhere. All this led up to him being a contender for the welter-weight championship fight. The match took place in 1936 at Earls Court. His opponent was Dave McCleare, three times ABA champion:

McCleare needed all his skill to withstand Chuck's attacks. Despite a valiant effort by Chuck in the final round when he did everything possible to snatch a last-minute victory, the title went to McCleare. A warm reception home from Chuck's friends in Barnsley was little compensation and instead of his weekly fight which had been his form since his career had started, Chuck took a thirteen week rest. In that period of rest, McCleare had lost his title to Scotsman Jake Kilrain. When Chuck felt ready to resume his career his come-back match was against the champion in a non-title bout. He lost on points. Chuck's career lasted another eighteen fights. Although there were one or two defeats, including one against Jack Lord of Bolton for the Northern area title, he won the majority.

It was heart-breaking for Chuck to give up the sport he loved. An operation for a detached retina in which he lost an eye, made him retire at 27. A career of 170 recorded fights plus many unrecorded in the boxing booths, had come to an end. After the war Chuck still kept an interest in boxing. He ran several boxing gyms, including one at his place of employment, Fox's steelworks at Stocksbridge, and Slazengers of Barnsley. Now happily retired, Chuck is still a popular figure in Barnsley, the town he never left, and deservedly has a place as one of Barnsley's well-loved sons.

Chuck Parker has passed on since this article was written. Ena recalled the last time that she ever saw him. 'It was at his home, a council flat at Worsbrough Common.' She'd knocked on the door, and when he answered he rubbed his eyes trying to make out who it was. Ena said that his sight was bad in his remaining eye but eventually he recognised her. After that he made such a fuss of her, made cups of tea and they talked about the old days. Ena recalled that she was really glad to have seen him and to have shared many happy memories. Shortly after, Chuck went to live at *Oaklands,* a residential home at Worsbrough Bridge, where he spent his last days.

Ena sighed and said, 'You know Annie, there were lots of young men living in the back-streets of Barnsley where I lived that were good at football and boxing. Most of them worked down the mines so it had to be a spare-time activity. I can recall quite a few besides Charlie Parker,' (Ena didn't call him Chuck), 'there was Charlie Hardcastle, Billy Jones, who's real name was Ely Exley, Lol Charlesworth and Jimmy Birch. Amongst the footballers that I can remember, around the streets where I lived were, three brothers, Alf, Jim and Wilf Slater, Charlie Scholey, 'Blink' Walker and George Skelly, who later became Alderman Skelly.'

Ena thought about the past. 'You know love, although times were hard, everybody knew everybody in those old terrace houses and we all pulled together. My mother would think I am living in a little palace now.' Ena gazed around her comfortable flat. She and her husband George raised four children, Stanley, Colin, Elaine and Annette, all who have their own children now. As she has said, 'What more could I want Annie?'

16. ROY KILNER

(1890–1928) Yorkshire and England Cricketer

MUCH has been written about Roy Kilner, the famous cricketer, but to satisfy myself, I needed to speak to someone who knew him personally. I was put in touch with Holroyd Oates, an elderly gentleman who could put me in the picture. Mr Oates was born at 23 Warley View, Halifax, in 1906, but in 1913 his parents left and went to live in Wombwell. I asked him how he came to know Roy Kilner. He replied that his auntie and Roy's mother were sisters, so there was a close family connection. Roy's father, Seth, was a publican and kept the *Half-Way House,* now known as the *White Rose Inn.* In fact, Mr Oates recollects spending his first Christmas at Wombwell in the living quarters above the pub, with all the members of the Kilner family. It was a huge family too. Roy's parents finished up with eleven children, seven boys and four girls. In the early days, before Seth had the pub, he was a sportsman, playing both cricket and football. He was also working at Mitchell Main Colliery.

Seth became good friends with Irving Washington, whose father was the manager of the pit. This resulted in Seth falling in love with Irving's sister, and marrying her. Her name was Mary Alice Washington. Roy Kilner was their second child. He was born 17 October 1890. Young Roy, as indeed all the Kilner boys, used to practise in the back yard of the *Half-Way House,* when the family lived there. Mr Oates mentioned that there was a bigger area then to knock the ball about in. Eventually, and with the encouragement of his father and Uncle Irving, Roy joined the cricket team at Mitchell's. He was fourteen. It was also noticed that he was a left-handed batter. This carried on until Roy reached the age of nineteen.People in the cricketing world were beginning to notice his expertise. This resulted in Roy being given a place in Yorkshire's second team. He was still playing for Mitchell's in his spare time. By the end of the summer, Roy had notched up 605 runs for them. This encouraged Yorkshire, in 1911, to place him in the Harrogate team. This in turn, culminated in Roy rising into first class cricket, but then came the start of the First World War. Roy enlisted and was sent to Colsterdale in North Yorkshire. The same year however, he returned to Wombwell, and married Annie Camplejohn. She was the third daughter of James Camplejohn, an engineer at Darfield Main.

In 1915, Annie gave birth to their first son, Roy junior. Roy the father, served with the 'Pals' during the war, and became caught up in the Battle of the Somme. During this time Roy's best friend, Major Booth, himself a good cricketer, was killed. Roy, too was injured, and had to come back to England to convalesce. By the end of the war, in 1918, Bernard Washington Kilner, Roy's elder brother, had also been killed, so it was a time of great sadness for Roy.

In 1919, Roy Kilner took up first-class cricket for Yorkshire again. He became very well known for his brilliant and confident batting. In 1920, Yorkshire played Derbyshire at Sheffield. Roy scored 206 runs not out (His previous best was against Gloucestershire in 1914. when he scored 169). This latest innings was his highest ever, and would prove to be the best of his career. Roy graduated from being an accomplished batter to a good all-rounder. He excelled in slow-spin left-arm bowling. In 1921, Annie gave birth to a second son, Major. By then, Roy and his wife were living at 212 Barnsley Road, fairly near to the *Half-Way House,* where he still practised his cricket in the yard.

Mr Oates said that one of the principal marks of Roy's character was his geniality. Always smiling, he was a very popular figure. He remembered a time when Roy's wife, Annie, told them a story about when he was playing in Australia. Someone shouted from the crowd, 'If you get him out, you can have a gold watch.' Apparently, Roy was successful, and did indeed receive the watch.

In 1922 Roy scored over a thousand runs, and delivered a thousand overs, taking a hundred wickets. This was a great 'double' and brought him to a new pinnacle of success. In the winter of 1924/25, he achieved the ultimate goal of being chosen to join the English team to tour Australia. In his first match he scored 103 runs against Western Australia. This proved to be his highest score for that season, but it was to no avail because their opponents won at the end of the tour by 307 runs. On 14 June 1924, Roy played for England against South Africa. The 1st Test was at Edgbaston. Surprisingly, he was dropped for the 2nd and 3rd, but recalled for the 4th at Old Trafford, where rain stopped play, so giving a dismal ending. 1925 brought the honour of Yorkshire being declared County Champions for the fourth year in succession, Surrey and Lancashire, second and third.

On 24 July 1926, Roy Kilner played his last match for England, against Australia at Old Trafford. Sadly, he was not in the final Test which resulted in a resounding victory for the home team. Roy carried on playing for Yorkshire, but unknown to him of course, he had played his final match for them. The venue was Scarborough, 31 August 1927. It was a good ending. In the first and second innings, he hit 43 and 51 respectively. Yorkshire won by eight wickets.

In the winter of 1927/28, Roy was invited to go to India by the Maharaja of Patiala, and coach the Rajendra Club in Punjab. He accepted the invitation, but the day after he set off, one of the men who had encouraged Roy throughout his career, his Uncle Irving, died. He was only forty-seven, and it was a great shock to Roy when he was told the news.

Unknowingly, Roy had picked a germ up in India, and by the time his engagement was over, and he was travelling back to England, he was very ill. When he arrived home, he was taken to Kendray Hospital, Barnsley. Roy was gripped with fever, and it came as a shock to everyone when he died the day before Good Friday, 5 April 1928. Wombwell's golden boy had gone.

Roy Kilner was buried on Tuesday 10 April, and over 100,000 people turned out to mourn him. A road in Wombwell was named in

The proud father Roy, pictured with his son, Roy Junior. *Photo, courtesy of Mick Pope, author of The Laughing Cricketer, and Hawke to Hutton Picture and Publishing services.*

honour of his memory. Mr Oates finished by saying, 'He was a good man, and a great cricketer, only thirty-eight when he died, cut off in his prime and sadly missed by everyone.'

Roy Kilner's Cricketing Statistics

Centuries

*206 Yorkshire v Derbyshire at Sheffield, 1920
169 Yorkshire v Gloucestershire at Bristol, 1914
166 Yorkshire v Northamptonshire at Northampton, 1921
150 Yorkshire v Northamptonshire at Harrogate, 1921
150 Yorkshire v Middlesex at Lord's, 1926
137 Yorkshire v Nottinghamshire at Nottingham, 1920
124 Yorkshire v Northamptonshire at Leeds, 1922
124 Yorkshire v Warwickshire at Dewsbury, 1925
121 Yorkshire v Warwickshire at Birmingham, 1920
120 Yorkshire v MCC at Lord's, 1919
117 Yorkshire v Worcestershire at Dudley, 1922
*115 Yorkshire v Gloucestershire at Leeds, 1919
113 Players v Gentlemen at Lord's, 1924
112 Yorkshire v Gloucestershire at Gloucester, 1919
104 Yorkshire v Leicestershire at Leeds, 1913
103 MCC v Western Australia at Perth, 1924/25
*100 Yorkshire v MCC at Scarborough, 1925
*NOT OUT

Century and six wickets in a match

113 and 6:20 Players v Gentlemen at Lord's, 1924
124 and 4:108 and 2:44 Warwickshire at Dewsbury, 1925

Ten wickets in a match

12:55 (5:18 and 7:37) Yorkshire v Sussex at Howe, 1924
11:48 (5:33 and 6:15) Yorkshire v Hampshire at Portsmouth, 1924
11:51 (5:29 and 6:22) Yorkshire v Essex at Harrogate, 1922
10:41 (2:15 and 8:26) Yorkshire v Glamorgan at Cardiff, 1923
10:66 (5:48 and 5:18) MCC v Victoria at Melbourne, 1924/25
10:90 (4:77 and 6:13) Yorkshire v Hampshire at Bournemouth, 1922
10:100 (4:78 and 6:22) Yorkshire v Surrey at Sheffield, 1923
10:116 (6:43 and 4:73) Yorkshire v Essex at Leyton, 1926
10:117 (2:77 and 8:40) Yorkshire v Middlesex at Bradford, 1926
10:153 (5:58 and 5:95) Yorkshire v Surrey at The Oval, 1924

Four catches in a match

5 Yorkshire v Northamptonshire at Northampton, 1924
5 Yorkshire v Essex at Leyton, 1926
4 Yorkshire v Somerset at Bradford, 1913
4Yorkshire v Hampshire at Bournemouth, 1922
4 MCC V West Indians at Barbados, 1925/26

The Double

Roy Kilner achieved the double of 1000 runs and 100 wickets in a season on three occasions (1922,1923, and 1926). Wilfred Rhodes (16), George Hirst (14) and Raymond Illingworth (6) are the only Yorkshiremen to have performed the double more often.

17. DICKIE BIRD

Yorkshire Batsman and International Umpire

HAROLD DENNIS BIRD, is a name of unfamiliar ring in Barnsley circles and throughout England. Mention however, Dickie Bird the umpire, and there will be instant recognition all over the world. You don't even have to be a cricket enthusiast to know about this 'son of Barnsley.' To be born in Church Lane, about a hundred yards from Barnsley Town Hall (to Ethel and James Harold), is a source of pride to Dickie. He has strong roots, and as he remarked, 'You can't get any closer than the town centre, the old Beckett Hospital was almost on the doorstep.' Born on 19 April 1933, Dickie was an enthusiastic child, and loved to spend his time kicking a ball around or playing cricket on rough ground in the area in which he lived. He went to school at Burton Road, and finished at Raley Secondary Modern, his sporting career starting in earnest at the latter, with his sports teacher 'Pop' Hudson being of great encouragment to the boys. As well as playing cricket and football for his school, young Dickie also appeared in the Barnsley Boys Football Team around the 1947 era.

In 1948, Dickie left school and started work in the fitters' shop at Monk Bretton Colliery. At the same time, he also played for Barnsley Cricket Club, based at Shaw Lane. He can clearly remember opening the innings with Mike Parkinson, another Barnsley personality who loved football and cricket, but is famous as a radio and television personality. Dickie was so successful in Barnsley Cricket Club, accumulating a great deal of runs, that when he reached nineteen years of age, he was invited to join the Yorkshire Colts as a batsman. Dickie left the pit, and from then on, followed the same way of life that he has today. In his own words, 'Living out of a suitcase.' He has never married, and one cause of regret to Dickie is that he has not raised a family. But hardly ever being at home would have been a huge drawback, and he would not have been able to pursue his career with the same veracity. He said that his sister, Marjorie, has been of tremendous support to him, doing his washing, cleaning, and looking after his house throughout the years. He had another sister, Sylvia, who unfortunately did not live beyond her early forties.

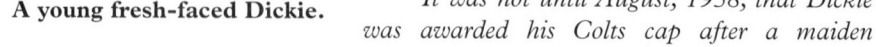

A young fresh-faced Dickie.

A piece from the *Barnsley Chronicle* about Dickie Bird, and written by Keith Lodge in 1962, ran:

In May, 1955, he was chosen to play for the Colts against Nottinghamshire Seconds at Shaw Lane after several earlier outings, and he thus became the first Barnsley player to play for the Colts at Shaw Lane since 1928, when Mr Clifford Hesketh and Harry Bedford were in the Yorkshire side. But unfortunately Dickie coming in at a crucial stage at number six, was out for a 'duck.' The match was however, eventually abandoned because of rain and snow.

It was not until August, 1958, that Dickie was awarded his Colts cap after a maiden century against Durham at Darlington, and a 92 v Cumberland at

Dickie keeps a watchful eye as ace Australian fast bowler, Len Pascoe powers the ball down the wicket in the 1977 tour of Australia.

Harrogate. He was the second Shaw Lane player to receive his Colt cap in post-war years, the other being wicket-keeper Eddie Leggard in 1957. Later the same month, Dickie played in his first full county championship match against Derbyshire at Leeds. Opening with Brian Stott, he stayed an hour for 10 in the first innings, sharing a partnership of 46. In the second innings he made five. Yorkshire won by 86 runs. That season Dickie played a big part in helping Yorkshire win the Minor Counties Championship, and still found time to top the Yorkshire League averages with 50.44.

In May of the following year, Dickie added one of the most glittering chapters to his career when he knocked an unbeaten 181 for Yorkshire at Bradford - his highest ever score - to help Yorkshire beat Glamorgan by an innings and 35 runs.

Dickie Bird was eventually signed by Leicestershire and did so well in the second team in the 1962 season, that a place was found for him in the County XI. Throughout his career in cricket, he has been noticed the most for his umpiring, a decision he took twenty-nine years ago. He has become quite a character out on the cricket pitch in his brilliant white umpire's coat. Easily drawn to emotion, he has a personality that endears him to many people, including our own Queen Elizabeth, who at the last count has had conversations with him twenty-seven times, mostly through her visits to the Test Matches, but Dickie has also been invited to lunch at Buckingham Palace. In June 1986, he became the proud recipient of an MBE (Member of the most excellent order of the British Empire), in the Queen's Birthday Honours List. He is a staunch royalist, and thinks that the Royal Family do a tremendous job for the country. Dickie has also had invitations to wine and dine at 10 Downing Street, and Chequers by Prime Ministers Margaret Thatcher and John Major.

During Dickie Bird's career in umpiring he has hosted 159 international matches, 67 of them being Test matches, 92 one-day international matches, 4 World Cup Tournaments, 3 World Cup Finals, and umpired all major cup finals throughout the world. Besides meeting leading figures in many different

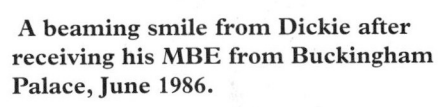

A beaming smile from Dickie after receiving his MBE from Buckingham Palace, June 1986.

1996. A proud moment for Dickie as he shows his Honorary Doctorate Degree from Sheffield Hallam University: for outstanding service to cricket.

countries, he has been honoured in his own. He very proudly accepted an Honorary Doctorate at Sheffield Hallam University in November 1996: for outstanding services to international cricket, and to cricket in general. Recently, and for the same reason, he also received an Honorary Doctorate in Law at Leeds University. 1996, saw him voted 'Yorkshireman of the Year,' and 1997, voted 'Yorkshire Personality of the Year.'

Dickie has retired from international umpiring, but still has a season to go before he stops umpiring county championship matches. His last circuit of the cricket season will take him up to the age of sixty-five, when he has to take full retirement which is the rule of the Cricket Board. Taking Dickie's character on board though, it is very difficult to imagine him sitting on the sidelines. He is a man who is absolutely dedicated to his chosen sport, and a fair minded person when it comes to crucial decisions. I asked him about his name, had he ever wanted to be called Harry. 'Not really,' he replied, 'at school, if you were named Clark, you would be known as 'Nobby,' if it was White, you would be 'Chalky,' so it stands to reason, with a name like Bird, 'Dickie' comes natural. Anyway, I think it's stood me in good stead, everybody remembers a name like mine.'

Dickie spoke of the changes that have been made in later years in cricket. He said that there is a vast amount of money coming in, as in any other sport these days. He thinks it rather sad, because the character has gone out of the game, and winning means everything. 'Don't get me wrong,' he remarked, 'everyone wants to win, but when the pleasure and enjoyment is lost, then you are finished.' I asked him, 'This may be a hypothetical question, but do you have any hobbies?' He smiled, 'Well actually, my relaxation comes on the cricket field, that is first and foremost, but at home I enjoy listening to records, my favourite singers being, Barbara Streisand, Nat King Cole and Shirley Bassey.' He is busy with his autobiography at the moment, having already written another three books, *Not Out, That's Out,* and *From the Pavilion End.* I was particularly impressed that he let me have an interview with him for my book, when he is very busy with his own.

Another of life's regrets for Dickie is that his parents did not live long enough to see him have such huge success as an umpire in the cricketing world. He spoke of his father working as a miner in the bowels of the earth from thirteen to sixty-five. He would have loved to have seen them both 'reight,' as many a Yorkshire person will understand. His own hard work has paid off. You have only to look at his seventeenth century cottage to appreciate this. It's the kind of house and grounds that suits Dickie, who is on call for a host of events. He leads a very busy lifestyle, but the cottage has an air of tranquillity about it. Dickie has had a very distinguished career, Barnsley people can be rightly proud of him, and although he has mixed with leaders of the world, he still possesses the 'common touch.'

HAROLD DENNIS 'DICKIE' BIRD, MBE
Test and World Cup Final Umpire

To date Dickie has umpired 159 International Matches including *Test Matches, World Cup Matches* and *One Day International Matches.*

Dickie has umpired the following:
Three *World Cup Finals* – West Indies v Australia at Lord's in 1975 West Indies v England at Lord's in 1979 – West Indies v India at Lord's in 1983.
Four *World Cup Tournaments*
The *Queen's Silver Jubilee Test Match* – England v Australia at Lord's in 1977.
The *Women's World Cup* in New Zealand in 1982
The *Women's World Cup Final* – England v Australia at Christchurch, New Zealand.
Thirty six *Major Cup Finals* all over the world including:-
Gillette Cup Finals, Nat West Cup Finals and *Benson & Hedges Cup Finals* all at Lord's.
The *Rothmans Cup* in Sharjah, U.A.E. 1983
Participating teams – Australia, Pakistan, India and England, and the *Final* – Pakistan v India.
The *Asia Cup* in Sharjah, U.A.E. in 1984
Participating teams – Pakistan, India and Sri Lanka.
The *Rothmans Cup* in Sharjah, U.A.E. 1985 between Pakistan, India and West Indies.
The 1985 *Asia Cup* in Sri Lanka between Pakistan, Sri Lanka and Bangladesh and the *Final* – Pakistan v Sri Lanka.

The *Champions Cup* in Sharjah between Pakistan, India, Sri Lanka and Bangladesh and the *Final* – Pakistan v Sri Lanka.
The finals for *The Best all Rounder in the World* and *The Best Batsman in the World* and also *The World Double Wicket Final.*
Umpired New Zealand v Pakistan *Test Series* in New Zealand 1994
Umpired Pakistan v Australia in Karachi 1994.
Umpired India v West Indies *Test Series* in India 1994.
Received *People of the Year Award* for outstanding service to cricket.
Also voted *Yorkshireman of the Yea*r same year 1996.
Awarded *Honorary Doctorate* at Sheffield Hallam University and *Honorary Doctorate of Laws* at Leeds University for outstanding service to cricket.
All the *Major Cup Quarter-Finals* and *Semi-Finals* in England
The *Bi-Centenary Test Match* – England v Rest of the World at Lord's (200 years MCC) in 1987.
A *Test Match* in Zimbabwe 1993 - Zimbabwe v New Zealand.
The *West Indies v Pakistan* Test Series in the West Indies 1993
1993 *Sharjah Tournament.*
Participating teams – West Indies, India, Sri Lanka and Pakistan.
Sixty seven *Test Matches* to date which is a world record.
Ninety two *One Day International Matche*s which is a world record.
Umpired Australia v Pakistan *Test Series* in Australia 1995.
In 1977 Dickie was voted *Yorkshire Personality of the Year.*
In June 1986 Dickie was made a *Member of the Most Excellent Order of the British Empire (MBE)* by Her Majesty Queen Elizabeth II in her Birthday Honours List.
Dickie played County Cricket for *Yorkshire CCC* and *Leicestershire CCC.*
Dickie has been appointed to the *World Cup Panel of Umpires* for 1987.
The *World Cup* played in India and Pakistan was Dickie's fourth World Cup Tournament.
Dickie turned down a tremendous amount of money by refusing to join Kerry Packer, also turning down a further sum of money to go on a rebel tour of South Africa – this was because of his loyalty to the established game which he was brought up with in Yorkshire and which has given him so much in life, also his loyalty to the Test and County Cricket Board.
Dickie has achieved every honour humanly possible in the umpiring world and has travelled all over the world.
Dickie is a fully qualified MCC Advanced Cricket Coach and a fully qualified MCC member.
Dickie is Honorary Life Member of Yorkshire County Cricket Club.
Dickie is the author of three best selling books titled *'Not Out', 'That's Out'* and *'From the Pavillion End'.*
He has been umpiring in First Class Cricket for 27 years. He played County Cricket for many years before he went into umpiring.
Umpired Australia v Pakistan *Test Series* in Australia 1996.

18. MARTYN DOUGLAS MOXON

Yorkshire and England Cricketer

MARTYN DOUGLAS MOXON'S mum, Audrey, invited me to her cosy flat in Monk Bretton to interview her famous son. Neither of them possess airs and graces, they were two friendly, down-to-earth people. His two young children, Charlotte, six, and Jonathan, three, were clambering all over him. Dad remonstrated, as fathers do, but it was clear to see the bond between this close-knit family. Martyn's own father, Derek, died in 1984, so he was not there for Martyn's marriage to Suzanne, in 1985, and the subsequent grandchildren, much to Martyn's regret. There had always been some element of sport in the Moxon family, Derek and his father before him, playing cricket and football locally. In fact,

St Helen's Junior School, Monk Bretton. Left: teacher Mr Rodgerson, Right: Headmaster Mr Taylor. Front row, seated on chairs, Martyn second left, Gordon Owen third left who eventually played football for Barnsley.

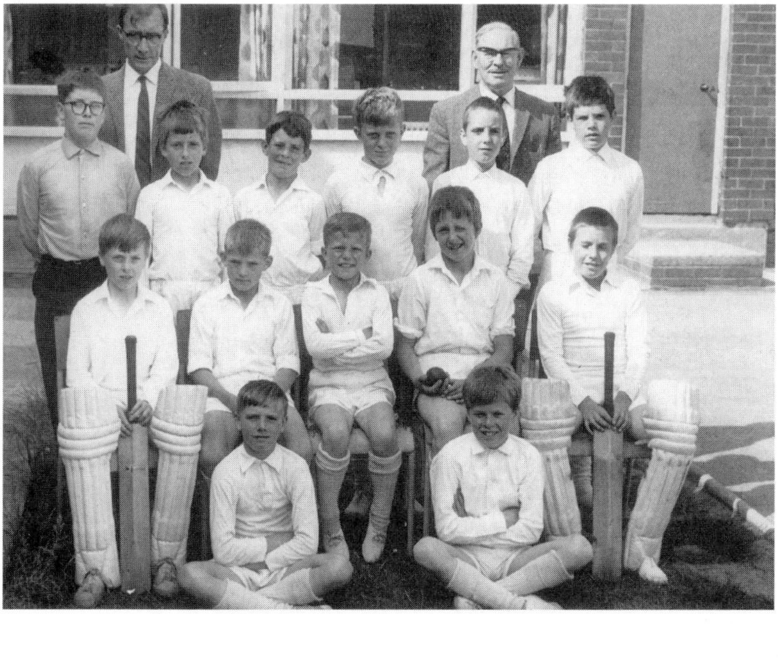

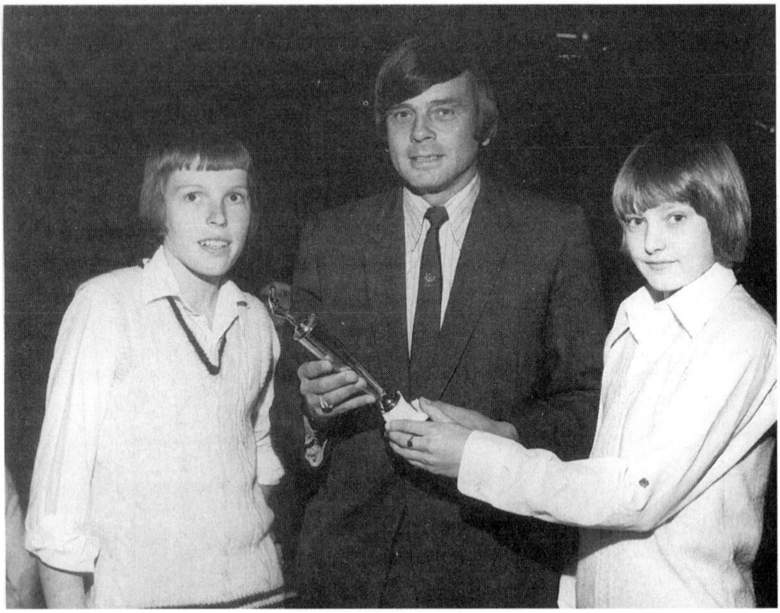

Presentation night at Wombwell Cricket Lovers Club. Left to right; Graham Higgins, Dickie Bird, Martyn Moxon.

Derek played in the Yorkshire League in his youth. Martyn is an only child, born on 4 May 1960. He went to St Helen's Infant and Junior School, Monk Bretton, and then on to Holgate Grammar School, staying until he was eighteen.

Educationally, Martyn did quite well, gaining eight 'O' levels, and three 'A' levels. He particularly enjoyed French, Geography and History. Leaving school, Martyn worked at a branch of Barclay's bank. Before all this however, he had played cricket and football continuously from being a youngster. Derek encouraged him, and by the time Martyn was nine, he was in the Barnsley Boys under eleven football team. He also played football for Holgate School in matches with other local schools. Martyn said that he might have taken football a bit further, but until the age of seventeen he was small in stature. He is now 6ft 1ins, so that is certainly not the case now. Cricket, however, was Martyn's first love, and he played for the Barnsley schools, and the Yorkshire under fifteens. The finals were usually held at Shaw Lane Cricket Ground. Martyn enjoyed his schooldays, particularly, the sixth form.

Whilst working at the bank, Martyn needed regular time off. He was playing in Yorkshire's Second Team, and Ray Illingworth, who

A recent photograph of the team of the Yorkshire County Cricket Club. Left to right:
Back row:
Chris Schofield, Colin Chapman, Gareth Batty, Alex Morris, Ryan Sidebottom, Paul Hutchinson, Ian Fisher, Matthew Wood.
Middle row:
Wayne Morton (Physio), Bradley Parker, Richard Stemp, Chris Silverwood, Alex Wharf, Gavin Hamilton, Anthony McGrath, Matthew Hoggard, Richard Kettleborough.
Front Row:
Darren Gough, Richard Blakey, Craig White, Michael Bevan, David Byas (Captain), Martyn Moxon, Peter Hartley, Mark Robinson, Michael Vaughan.

was manager of the team, negotiated with Barclay's for time off. This carried on until Martyn was twenty, when he knew that he had to decide between banking or cricket. He chose cricket, and in 1980, signed full-time with Yorkshire at the Headingley Ground.

Martyn's first two winters were spent in South Africa. Mainly, he was the opening batsman, right-hand bat, and right-arm bowler. For the first three years after signing he was in Yorkshire's Second Team, depending on whether or not Geoff Boycott was playing. Martyn would take Geoff's place if the occasion arose. In his first two, three-day Championship games for Yorkshire in 1981, he was the first player in a very long time to make centuries in both games. The first, and also his debut, against Essex at Headingley resulted in a score of 116 runs, the second was against Derbyshire, with a score of 111. This was a very good start, and in 1984 Martyn was made a permanent member of the First Team, and played the whole season. He was picked for the England team against the West Indies, but the day before the Test Match, he had to disappointingly pull out, due to a broken rib sustained in a match at Northampton.

Eventually, Martyn, made his Test debut in 1986, and four years later, in 1990, he became Captain of the Yorkshire Team. He has

Martyn (with cricket bat) when playing for Monk Bretton Under 18's.

travelled extensively throughout his career, to places such as, India, Australia, Sri Lanka, New Zealand, South Africa, West Indies, Canada and Zimbabwe. He now suffers back pain, to such an extent that he no longer bowls. This is due to stress fractures, and is a problem that flares up now and again.

I asked Martyn if he had admired any sporting personality in the past and was given the reply that his favourite had been Alan Ball, the footballer. Martyn's own relaxation away from the cricket field is

Martyn Moxon

Batting Career

First Class							
M	**I**	**NO**	**RUNS**	**H**	**50s**	**Ct**	**AV**
305	523	47	20,572	44	111	215	43.21
Sunday League							
149	141	8	4,114	3	24	46	30.93
Benson and Hedges							
47	47	7	1,766	2	13	19	44.15
Nat West							
31	31	6	1,208	2	9	12	48.32

Bowling

First Class				
Ov	**M**	**R**	**WKTS**	**AV**
441.4	73	1,481	28	52.89
Sunday League				
164	3	868	21	41.33
Benson and Hedges				
57	1	242	9	26.88
Nat. West				
22	6	68	4	17.00

golf. He also likes to relax with his wife by going to the cinema, or taking her out for dinner, in the Wetherby area where they both live. 'Had he any ambitions for his children?' I asked. He said that if either of them were interested in sport, he would encourage it, but he would never try to force them because their happiness was more important. Paramount to Martyn, is for them both to have a decent education. As for his own ambitions, he would like to win another Yorkshire County Championship Trophy, and when he has finished playing, to take up coaching. I feel sure that Martyn Douglas Moxon, will accomplish whatever he sets out to do.

Walking for the Killingbeck Children's Heart Surgery Fund. Martyn with his daughter, Charlotte, with Wayne Morton and daughter Lauren.

19. ALEXANDER CORFIELD MORRIS

Barnsley and Yorkshire Cricketer

ALEXANDER CORFIELD MORRIS was born on 4 October 1976, to Chris and Janet. His home is in the Old Town district of Barnsley. Alex is a happy looking curly-headed lad of 6ft 4ins, easy to talk to. He has one younger brother, Zachary Clegg Morris, born 4 September 1978, who is also a cricketer. I remarked that their names were rather unusual, and Alex replied that they were family names, Corfield being the middle name from the grandfather on his father's side, and Clegg, the middle name from the grandfather on mother's side. The boys' father, Chris is a professional singer. He performed under the name of Lance Fortune, whilst living in London in 1960, making a hit record, *Be Mine.* In 1963, he teamed up with a band from Cornwall, called The Staggerlees, but were based in Sheffield. It was in Sheffield that Chris met Janet, a Barnsley lady, they married and then had their

Alex with the under 14's, Oundle, 1991. *Left to right,*
Back row: **Vickram Solanki, Richard Newell, Phillip Ayres, Kevin Innes, Simon Horsfall,**
Front row: **Phillip Neville, Paul Collingwood,Alex Morris, Lee Marland, Neil Killeen, Christie McDonald, Anarag Singh.**

Barnsley Boys Football Team, under 11's, 1988/89. *Left to right, Back row:* **Karl Baker, Mark Narey, Mark Haran, John Day, Alex Morris, Mark Whittaker, Paul Smith, Paul Reeves.**
Front row: **Dean Fitzpatrick, John Woofinden, Andy Gregory, Mark Hurst, Jason Blunt, Mark Walley, Daren Utley.**

two sons. These days, Chris sings in a duo, Stag and Lee, with Tony Grigg.

Alex can remember happy days spent on the beaches in Guernsey and Cornwall playing football and cricket with his father. He said Chris was a source of encouragement to both boys. The local school was at Wilthorpe, with Alex finally making his way to Holgate Comprehensive, and then Barnsley College. Mr Middleton, the sports teacher at Wilthorpe could also see the potential in Alex. In his days at Holgate, Alex gained GCSE's in Sports Studies, Business Studies, English and Maths. In college he chose Sports Science. He still played football and cricket, depending upon the season. Alex became a junior soccer player (goalkeeper) with the Barnsley Boys at Oakwell, but admitted that he was not very good at it, so cricket became his chosen sport. He started at Barnsley Cricket Club, helped out with Chris, his dad, Steve Oldham and Arnie Sidebottom.

Alex signed a contract for the Yorkshire Academy of Cricket based at Bradford. He was still at college, so could only go in part-time, but it was valuable experience. He is a left-hand bat, and a right arm medium bowler. Playing locally for Barnsley, and school cricket with Yorkshire under 11s, 13s and 15s, has taught Alex all-round skills. He then represented England in the Under Seventeens. This was followed by playing in the West Indies with the England Under Nineteens in 1994/95, and Zimbabwe 1995/96. His brother Zachary is now touring with the Under Nineteens. Alex has also played in the Hong Kong 'sixes,' a small team of six players, captained by Mike Watkinson. To date, at the time of this interview (1996), Alex had made his official debut for Yorkshire's First Team, with a score of 48 runs. A very promising start for such an important first game. The rest of the year was with Yorkshire's Seconds, his highest score being 175. Alex mentioned that in the run-up to the cricket season, which usually starts 1 April, there is intensive pre-season training. He keeps himself fit from September to April, but shortly before I saw him, he

Alex signing for Yorkshire in 1994. Left to right, Chris Morris (Dad), Steve Oldham, Alex Morris, Doug Padgett, Zac Morris (Brother).

had trained for three weeks in Zimbabwe.

I asked Alex if there was anyone he particularly admired in the cricket game. He replied, 'Ian Botham.' He also mentioned that he was a friend of Ian's son, Liam, who plays cricket and rugby. Although he is making his career in cricket, Alex still loves a game on the soccer field.

Alex is making headway in the cricketing world. He is a young man with a good future ahead of him, and another Barnsley sports star in the making.

Alex Morris

Batting Career

First Class Championship (Yorkshire)			
Games	**Runs**	**HS**	**AV**
5	97	40	17
2nd XI Bain Hogg			
14	392	116	31
2nd XI Championship			
24	951	172	36
Sunday League			
8	99	48 *not out*	*20*

Bowling

First Class Championship (Yorkshire)		
Wks	**Best**	**AV**
2	1–16	
2nd XI Bain Hogg		
8	1–8	
2nd XI Championships		
30	4–6	
Sunday League		
4	2–18	2.19

20. SPORTING HEROES

Of Rockley Mount and Laithes Lane Day Centre

ROCKLEY MOUNT SCHOOL is situated in a semi-rural area of Barnsley, surrounded by fields near Kingstone, and provides a happy environment for the disabled youngsters who attend each day. Besides the ordinary academic lessons, the school has an enviable record of sporting achievements won by the pupils, notably, throwing the discus, club, and slalom events.

Mrs Veronica Kay, a teacher who has been at the school for the past fifteen years, explained to me how the young athletes are chosen for the team that represents Yorkshire in the Nationals. All the participating schools in the Yorkshire area go along to Thornes Park in Wakefield for preliminary selection. There are various degrees of disability, so the children are classified into different sections to make it fairer. For example, in precision club, all competitors who can stand, are furthest from the target. Next in line come the manual wheelchair users, and lastly, the electric wheelchair users. There are also varying degrees of how limbs are affected, the most handicapped being the quadriplegics. Limitations are classified by the physiotherapists, the two at Rockley Mount being Mrs Pat Barraclough and Mrs Lynn Newman. She explained that also, some of the children may have impaired vision. All these things lead to careful selection of events entered, timing and distance.

One common denominator amongst all the children though, is a staunch heart. Amidst all the excitement, they do their level best on competition day at Thornes Park. Smiling faces accompany their eagerness to do well, and their determination to overcome all obstacles. On 1 May 1996, twenty-one pupils were selected from Rockley Mount School to go to Wakefield. This led to nine of them being selected for the British Sports Association for the Disabled, in the National Championships to be held at Stanley Park, Blackpool, starting the first Saturday in July, 1996. This was a proud moment for their headmaster, Robert Sharples.

Lynn Newman, Veronica Kay and Pat Barraclough at Rockley Mount School.

The results for the National

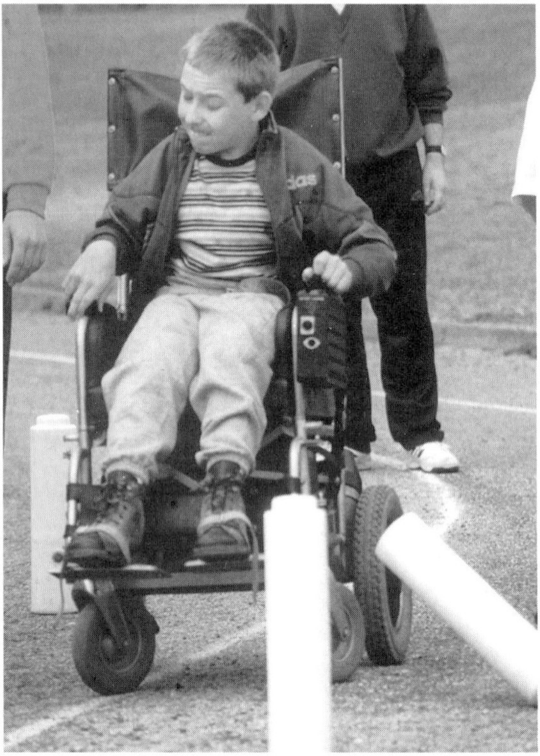

Above: **Richard Kay negotiating the slalom at the inter-house games, July 1996.**

Left: **Louise Dodgson throwing the frisbee in the inter-house games, July 1996.**

Below: **Sheer determination. Gavin Godfrey, BSAD National Games, Blackpool, July 1996**

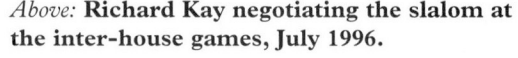

Championships were as follows:

Dale Tansley: 400 metres, bronze; shot, gold;relay, silver; 200 metres, gold.

Gavin Godfrey: shot, bronze; 100 metre, gold; relay, silver; 200 metres, silver.

Alison Clark: 60 metres, gold; relay, bronze; slalom, gold (new national record).

Angela Taylor: 100 metres, silver; shot, silver; discus, bronze.

Nicola Meigh: 60 metres, silver; distance club, gold;

Helen Dickinson: precision club, gold; distance club, gold (new national record).

Richard Kay: relay, bronze; precision club, silver.

Gareth Bould: distance club, gold.

Jamie Campbell: 100 metres, silver; 200 metres, gold (new national record).

All in all, an impressive total of 10 gold, 8 silver, and 5 bronze medals.

Helen Dickinson throwing the club at the BSAD Blackpool National Junior Games, July 1996.

A further achievement was accomplished last year by a young girl who lives in Wakefield, but attends Rockley Mount. Her name is Rebecca Nicholson, and she was born on 11 July 1985. 'Becky' suffers from cerebral palsy, and Williams Syndrome. She wanted to raise money for local hospices around the West Yorkshire area. She wrote to Wakefield High Security Prison to ask for sponsorship for an eleven-mile bike ride, from Wakefield Hospice to the Prince of

Scott Grain throwing the club in the inter-house games, July 1996.

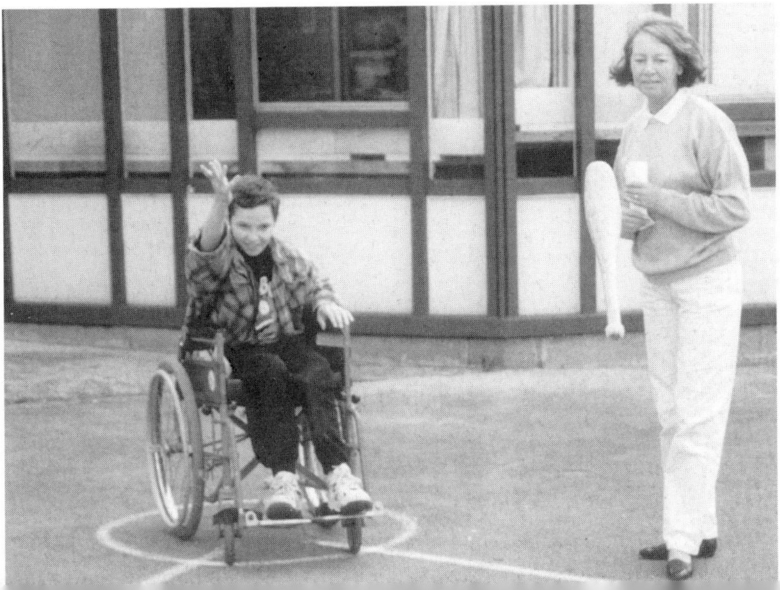

Wales Hospice in Pontefract. The prisoners responded by running 14 miles within the prison grounds, and raising £315 in the process. Rebecca's mother added that they also presented her with a beautifully hand-crafted wooden jewellery box for Rebecca's personal use. She completed the journey, using a specially adapted four-wheel cycle that she had to pedal. This took place on 8 September 1996. She received many congratulations, amongst them, a letter from the Queen, from Princess Diana, from the Prime Minister, and from Al Fayed, the owner of Harrod's store in London. Altogether, she raised just under £1,900. A great effort for a courageous little girl. The money was divided between six hospices within the West Yorkshire area. John Major presented Rebecca with a trophy, for the 'Child of Achievement' award.' A fitting honour.

Two former Rockley Mount pupils, have represented their country in national and international events. I interviewed them both at Laithes Lane Day Centre. Both have Spina Bifida and Hydrocephalus. I first spoke to Gareth Wood, from Honeywell, Barnsley, born 2 November 1973. Gareth has been highly successful in wheelchair athletics, shot-put, discus, and slalom events. From the age of ten Gareth was greatly encouraged by Pat Barraclough and Veronica Kay at his former school. As a junior in 1989, he was chosen with a team of twenty-six others to represent Great Britain in the international events at the Orange Bowl Stadium in Miami. He was entered in the 100 metres dash, the shot-put, and the slalom, a competition whereby the contestant has to quickly wheel his way in and out of cones. In most of the events Gareth came in fifth or sixth place, not bad considering that in the slalom alone there were representatives from twenty-five different countries. He didn't see a

Smiling Rebecca Nicholson with her certificate, London, 5 February 1997.

Becky's bike.

great deal of Miami itself, because training came first. They would have a four-course meal at the end of the day at the hotel, and then go to bed and prepare for the next day. Gareth said that it was an uplifting sight when thousands of visitors were settled in their seats, an occasion that he won't forget.

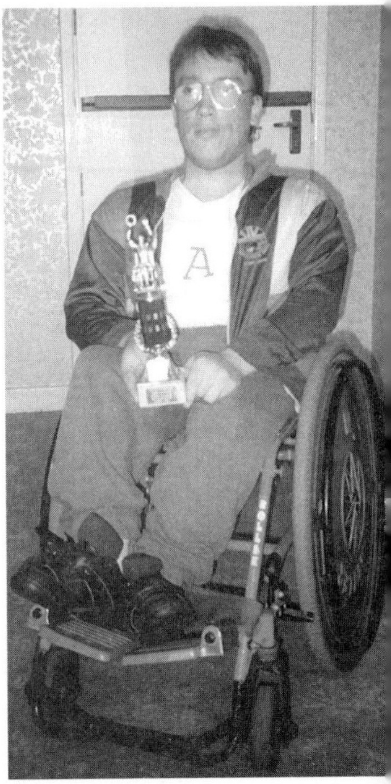

Gareth Wood. Taken at Laithes Lane Day Centre, 1996.

Gareth has also done mountain climbing. He has the Rockley House Trust trophy for climbing Ben Nevis (4,406ft). Three climbers were selected to climb the highest mountain in England, Scotland and Wales. The other two which were scaled by the disabled, were Scafell Pike (3,210ft) and Snowden (3,560ft). This was in May, 1989. Gareth said that the climbing was done in special chairs, and they were contacted by radio every ten minutes in case they got into difficulty. They also had army back-up, any trouble and they would have been called out. I asked Gareth if he'd had any qualms about it, but he laughed and said that he had practised first on other mountains. 'What was it like on the top,' I asked. 'Rocks,' he replied, 'covered by three feet of snow.'

'Had he any hobbies,' I asked. Apparently he likes to go for a drink, he plays basketball, and he fishes. One of his favourite spots being the Fleets which is quite near to Honeywell. He likes to fish with 'Cleggy' (Dick Clegg), the well-known angler, and as Gareth put it, 'like a brother to me.' At this point, I spoke to Andrew Quashie, Gareth's friend, and a competitor like himself, but in the field of snooker. Andrew was born on 12 June 1965, at Cudworth. He has represented Yorkshire in the Nationals at the John Spencer Snooker Club in Sterling, Scotland. Andrew has qualified twice for this event. He has not won so far, but it has been an honour to be selected. Recently, he competed at Lincoln and won a trophy and a snooker cue to add to his collection, but the match that he enjoyed most as a spectator, was an exhibition between Jimmy White and Ronnie O'Sullivan at the Metrodome. Andrew is the secretary of the Barnsley Destroyers, a wheel-chair basket-ball team based at the Metrodome, Barnsley. He and

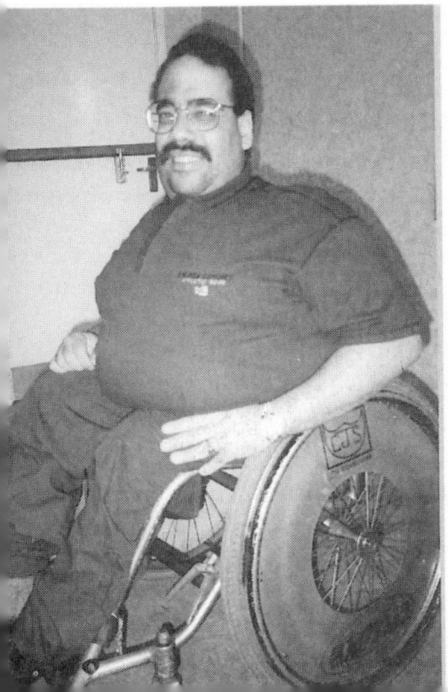

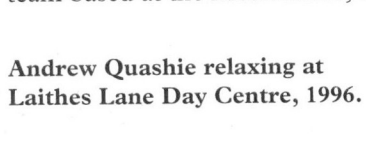

Andrew Quashie relaxing at Laithes Lane Day Centre, 1996.

Robert Stendall in his office at Laithes Lane Day Centre.

Gareth play every week, and the team have been practising for four years.

Mr Robert Stendall, manager of the Day Centre commented, 'Everyone here is adult, there isn't much in the way of sporting facilities so usually our pupils go to the Metrodome.' He also mentioned that there are a vast range of disabilities to cater for, from the profoundly disabled, to people who have severe epilepsy. Some also have learning difficulties, but others are very academic. One of their day visitors has eight 'O' levels and two 'A' levels. 'This is where the challenge comes in for the staff,' he remarked, 'but we find the work to be most rewarding.' I asked the manager if he was a Barnsley man. He replied that he was born in Rotherham, but his ancestors, in 1380, came from the village of King's Sterndale, in North Derbyshire. 'Hence my name, Mr Stendall.'

I found my visit to the two centres to be illuminating and I think that Barnsley has some remarkable 'sporting heroes.'

British Sports for the Disabled National Championships, 1996. Left to right, *Back row:* **Dale Tansley, Gavin Godfrey, Angela Taylor, Claire Ward, Nicola Meigh, Jamie Campbell.** *Front row:* **Helen Dickinson, Gareth Bould, Louise Dodgson, Richard Kay.**

21. GLEN HAIGH

Weight-Lifter and European Champion

I MET GLEN HAIGH, a disabled weight-lifter at his home in Kendray. A pleasant young man who has done well at his chosen sport. Glen was born at 42 Lambert Road, Kendray on 28 August 1963. His parents are Brian and Marlene, and he has a brother named Glyn.

Glen suffers from spina bifida. He has shown great courage from birth by enduring more than forty operations to strengthen his spine and the insertion of a metal rod to keep him upright. Glen went to Rockley Mount School, the focus of his earliest sporting memory, where he and other pupils and teachers visited Stoke Mandeville. Glen was thirteen at the time. This visit inspired him to enter competitions himself, and for the next few years he did wheelchair racing, discus throwing and snooker, winning medals and trophies in the process. He also had the encouragement of Kevin Dawson, one of the teachers. These were junior events, and it wasn't until Glen was sixteen and had joined Pinderfield's Paraplegic Fellowship Club, a sports club at Wakefield, that he took the competitions more seriously.

In the beginning, weight-lifting was a way of keeping himself fit, but after a while he found himself to be strong enough to enter the Senior National Championships at Stoke Mandeville. After two to three years of self-improvement and winning more trophies, he was invited to join the International Squad. I asked Glen how the movement of lifting is performed. He explained that he has to lie on a flat bed, with the weights resting on racks one inch above chest level. The weights are then lifted up to full arm extension and held. I said, 'What would happen if you dropped it'? He laughed and replied, 'It would hurt. Actually though, that has happened to me in training, but on a competition bench it's not possible because of the racks. This sort of thing can be anticipated.'

Marlene and Brian helped and encouraged their son with his training, and by the time that Glen was twenty-two, he could lift 90 kilos, nearly twice his own body weight. He had been weight-training for five years by this time and was entered into his first international contest in France. The year was 1988. Glen received a specially - adapted wheelchair from the Prince's Trust, and the Barnsley Spina

Glen demonstrates the bench press at Hoyland Sports Centre.

Bifida Association. He came third in the competition. It was around this time, that Glen said that power-lifting started to take the place of weight-lifting. He had met the Weight-Lifting World Champion, Ralph Rowe, at Stoke Mandeville, and he had shown Glen the new lifting technique. Whilst the body is stretched out flat, the racks holding the weights are above and behind the athlete's head. The arms are lifted, the weights are grasped, and with the guidance of a 'catcher', (the person helping) the weight is removed from the racks and brought to full arm extension. The lifter gets the weight under control, lowers it to chest height, and on the referee's signal, the athlete lifts and holds the weight.

In 1989, Councillors Dick Shirt, and Harry Wilson, presented Glen with a cheque from the Barnsley Council Leisure Amenities, to help with his expenses for training and travelling. They said that the town of Barnsley were very proud of him. In this same year, Glen was asked to compete in Poland for the Disabled European Weight-lifting Championships. His personal best by now was 120 kilos. This was achieved at Hoyland Sports Centre at his weekly training sessions. This was also only 5.5 kilograms off the world record for a disabled person. In the actual competition, Glen came fifth. He was disappointed, but it was still a tremendous achievement out of all Europe. If he had equalled his own training record, then he would have come third, taking the bronze medal, but the actual trip to

Poland took seventeen hours, with a long car journey to follow, so it was rather gruelling before the competition had even started. Upon Glen's return, and later in the year, he was presented with a training bench by Mr Vic Paynter, managing director of Lyons Cakes, Monk Bretton. Glen was delighted with the gift, and settled down to train for the 1990 World Championships for the Disabled at Assen, Holland. They were held from the twelfth to the twenty-sixth of July. The invitation came from the headquarters of the British Les Autres Sports Association based in London.

Glen's training by now was being undertaken by Roy Garner, an international coach who lived in Rugby. He had his own gym, and once a month the international squad used to go to his house and practise under his leadership. Glen came third at Assen, taking the bronze medal, with a lift of 110 kilos, a great honour for Britain.

The next major event that Glen hoped to fulfil was the Paralympics, which in 1992 were to be based in Spain. He and his disabled weight-lifting friend, Gerard Belcher of Shafton, had both fulfilled the qualifications needed to enter, but when the teams were picked, the British selectors only chose three out of the ten selected body weights because of cash cutbacks, therefore the two British champions were not included in the final selections. This decision was a bitter blow to the two Barnsley men. Glen said that he felt truly sickened by this after training for the fours years leading up to it.

Life goes on though, and Glen decided to take the setback in true sports fashion and carry on training in the hope that he would be included in the next Paralympics to be held at Atlanta, in 1996. These hopes too were dashed, because in 1995 Glen's blood pressure became too high for him to carry on doing competition work. This was a great disappointment, because he was subsequently gaining in strength as the years went by. He had already lifted the equivalent of a sixteen stone person in 1990 when he took the silver in the British National Championships. Glen himself only weighed 9st 9lbs. He has picked up many trophies and medals along the way, including a gold, when once again he lifted in the British National Championships in 1993 at Wolverhampton. He has travelled to France, Belgium and Holland during his career. At the moment Glen works for the Social Services at *Regent House,* Barnsley. He enjoys a quiet drink at the week-end, usually at the Central Working Men's Club at Kendray. I asked him what his future plans were. He said that he had been thinking of taking coaching up, and perhaps putting some youngster on the road to success. Glen is a modest man and doesn't openly boast of his achievements, in fact it was his friend, Gerard Belcher, or 'Gez', as he likes to be called, who told me about him, but I am sure that whatever path Glen takes, he will make a success of it.

1991 members of the British Team at the World Championships being photographed at Assen in Holland. Left to right, *Back row:* **Gordon Steven, Patrick O'Malley, Tony Bishop.** *Front row:* **Chris Bantin, Roy Garner** *(International coach),* **Glen Haigh.**

22. RIDING FOR THE DISABLED ASSOCIATION

Barnsley Group

THE DISABLED RIDING CENTRE is based on twelve-and-a-half acres of land by the side of what used to be Barnsley's old cattle market and abattoir at Pontefract Road. Finding the entrance which was marked by the sign, RDA (Riding for the Disabled Association), I wound my way up the long road leading to the office, looking for Mrs Pat O'Connell, the group organiser. Taking me on an extensive tour of the grounds, I was surprised at the size of the area. It was a beautiful day and I could see the attraction of anyone wishing to ride a horse there. Pat is an energetic lady with lots of enthusiasm. She was born in 1938 and has had two children. Her elder child, Penelope, died in 1975 after being kicked by a horse. Her son, Ian, was born in 1979, the same year that RDA came into being. Pat became involved with them as a volunteer helper, her baby son spending his time asleep in his carrycot in the corner of a field. Pat said that if their daughter had lived, then she would have been brain-damaged, and because she loved horses so much, then they would have used the services of a disabled riding school. She remarked that she feels that she is giving something that her daughter would wish her to do.

Originally, the Barnsley RDA rode at a local riding school, paying half the normal riding school rates and taking two groups, one from a Day Care Centre, and one from a Special School. A second riding school was used when another school wanted to come riding. The demand for the service offered by the RDA began to escalate, and the group got to the point where they could no longer afford to extend any further. Then, in 1981, South Yorkshire County Council and Barnsley Council launched the Dearne Valley Reclamation Scheme, a plan to clean up and use the derelict land within the Dearne Valley. Interested groups were invited to apply for the use of areas of this land, an offer the Barnsley RDA was quick to pick up. In October 1983, a lease was signed, and the fund-raising began in earnest. When SYCC began to landscape the Barnsley Main spoil heap, top soil was removed, 'slag' placed there, top soil put back and the whole area re-seeded. Their daughter's old pony *Brandy*, which had been at a riding school at Rotherham was returned, and the new centre was started.

In 1984, planning permission was sought for buildings. It was

Mrs Pat O'Connell with one of the pupils, Ben Fyfield sitting astride his best friend, Heidi.

granted, and things got under way. One young man, Barry, whose wife Marie, had two ponies which came on loan to the RDA,worked for a heavy plant hire company. They were kind enough to lend a JCB out most weekends providing that Barry was the one to drive it. He set about the levelling of the road and the site where the stable block was to be built. Pat said that the local goodwill was wonderful. Barnsley firms helped a great deal by donating used bricks, tiles, and timber, etc. Other firms offered materials at cost price, and in many cases with a discount. The actual building work itself was done as a training exercise by the CVS Community Programme, which employed mainly young people who were supervised by extremely well qualified staff.

As the winter of 1984 approached, and the number of ponies either owned by, or loaned to the group, grew, the CVS Community Programme offered to provide staff to teach riding, and to care for the ponies. The first staff at the Oakwell Centre were appointed, their wages met by the Community Programme, so that all funds raised by the RDA group could go into funding the building, or in caring for the ponies. After Community Programme finished, the group had to meet the cost of paying a Stables Manager as well as the cost of keeping the stables running, and feeding and caring for the ponies. Since the building of the stables, an all-weather riding arena, a classroom, and temporary storage have been added. The land has been landscaped to provide a flat grassed riding area, and a driving/riding track has been laid around the whole site. Many trees, shrubs, and flowering plants have been added to enhance the appearance.

At present the stables own eight horses: *Rosy, Fitz, Bobby, Heidi, Spotty, Amber, Lady,* and *Peter*. *Brandy* is no longer here, crippled with osteo-arthritis, so he had to be humanely 'put down'. Pat said the ponies are treated like family pets, but keeping them is very expensive. In summer, they just eat grass and a little hay, but in winter, the feed bill is staggering. Their teeth have to be rasped every year, because they never stop growing. They go down in winter with coughs and chills like any human, but Pat remarked that the Stable Managers, Davina Leech and Janet Clayton, try to keep the outgoings as low as possible. Nevertheless, the bills, inclusive of water, electricity and telephone, come to a yearly total in excess of £15,000. 'All this has to be found through voluntary effort. The rent paid to Barnsley Council is a peppercorn one, and we don't pay rates, so that's a great help,' Pat concluded.

We spoke at length about the pupils, eighty disabled in all use the facilities each week, their ages ranging from three upwards. *Heidi* is a Shetland pony and is used for the very small children. A lady named Muriel used to ride the horses. When she was in her sixties she went blind. Having loved horses all her life, she took up riding at the stables. Muriel used to be taken to the stables by Barnsley's Dial-a-Ride service. Her words to Pat were, 'It's a bit of a bugger love, when you get to my age and you've to do something that you always wanted to do when you were a bairn.' Pat said that she was a wonderful, independent lady, and she loved being amongst the youngsters who used to pull her leg a lot. When she died, in her seventies, she was very much missed.

Another young lady, suffering from cerebral palsy, is a regular visitor. She is blind, deaf, and cannot sit because she has no muscle tone. She spends most of her time sitting on a bean bag. Her sense of smell is heightened, and when she nears the stables, she squeals with delight. Pat explained that the staff have to take the saddle off and gently lay her on the horse's back. She then wraps her arms lovingly around it's neck. She has a great affinity with the horses, and cries when it's time to leave. Medical consent is needed for every disabled rider at the centre, and they never go out with the horses unless they are accompanied by an able-bodied person, and in some cases, two or three helpers are needed. There are a wide spectrum of disabilities to cater for. Pat mentioned that Downs Syndrome children are a joy to be with. They have one little boy who is autistic, and refuses to talk to humans. He will only converse through *Bobby* the horse who nods his head and paws the ground. If anyone needs to ask the youngster a question, it is spoken through *Bobby*.

Three shows a year are allowed, so the stables take advantage of this as a way of raising funds. They also have a Christmas gymkhana purely for fun. Everyone wears fancy hats, and prizes are usually rosettes and Mars bars. They have hot drinks, soup, and orange juice, and it lasts all morning. Parents are invited too, but turn-out has been disappointing, Pat commented. The children and the voluntary helpers all get a great deal of fun out of it however.

A few years ago, someone fired the stables when it was dark and deserted. The horses were freed, but a chilling note was left behind saying, 'This time we let the animals out, next time you might not be so lucky. You will find the cart floating in the Dearne.' This was a small cart that was used in the shows. No-one was ever prosecuted for this demonic action, and it was another set-back of course. Pat also added, 'More recently, 12 five-barred wooden field gates, with chains and padlocks had been stolen, worth over £1,500. Money the RDA cannot afford to pay for what is just wanton vandalism.' I asked Mrs O'Connell of her hopes for the future. She said that they may one day, have an indoor riding school, new roads, a proper office, living accommodation for a caretaker, and a suitable holder for hay and straw storage. With her determination, and the backing of the committee, I feel sure that the rest of their plans will come true.

The riding stables with Davina in the foreground.

23. BRIAN STONES

Weight-Lifter and Paralympic Gold Medallist

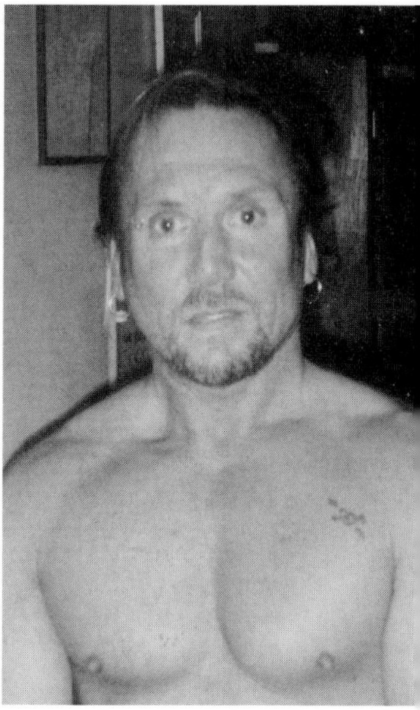

MY FIRST meeting with Brian Stones was at his home at Penistone. He is an independent man and has overcome great adversity in life. Brian was born in the Smithies area to Sidney and Winnie. Living in the area myself over thirty years ago, I could remember Brian as a child, living with his family of five sisters and a brother. He related that his father played professional football for Barnsley and York City. Brian too was interested in football, playing for Raley Secondary Modern. In later years, after leaving school, he played for the Athersley Arms, Lundwood, and other local teams, hoping to make football his career.

In the early seventies, Brian met and married a young woman named Lynda. They settled in Penistone and had a little girl, Keri Danielle. Everything was going brilliantly for Brian and Lynda, he had obtained work at Hepworth's Iron Company, and they were buying a house. About ten weeks after starting his job, and eight weeks after their daughter was born, Brian suffered severe injury. He was coming home from work on his scooter, when he hit a hole in the road. He was thrown off his bike, and into the path of a car. Brian said, 'the driver panicked and reversed back onto me.' This accident resulted in Brian sustaining multiple chest injuries, and a back broken in two places. He was given two days to live, his young wife, aged twenty at the time, enduring the trauma. Miraculously, Brian survived and spent the next nine months in Lodge Moor Hospital, Sheffield, repairing both mentally and physically. His injuries had left him suffering from paralysis and having to use a wheelchair.

For the next two years, Brian built up his stamina by going to the gymnasium at the Sports Club at Lodge Moor, and practising swimming, table-tennis and various other activities. Because he was of stocky build, weight-lifting became a natural. Gradually, Brian started to represent his club, first in local events, and then elsewhere throughout the country. He did so well at national level that he was then selected as part of the British team. In his own words, 'I was

1976. The European Championships in Paris. Brian presses 303lbs to become silver medalist.

dead chuffed.' I asked him exactly what the bench press entails. He explained that the athlete lies flat on the bench, locks hands with the bar, lifts and holds until the referee says 'down.' There are three lifts allowed. Brian also said that the able-bodied have a distinct advantage over the disabled by the fact that their legs can 'dig in.' He carried on by saying that the keynote is to have a determined attitude, never give in.

In 1976 Brian qualified for the European Championships, held in Paris. With a bench press of 303lbs, he took the silver medal in the feather-weight section, his body-weight being 8 stones. He also remembers being very nervous. It was in the mid-1970s that Brian met a man whom he admired, Arnold Schwarzeneggar, film star. He had succeeded in becoming Mr Universe for the sixth time. After

Photographed in the mid-1970s at Leeds. Brian with screen hero, Arnold Schwarzenegger.

Arnie had given a talk about nutrition, he approached Brian and they talked about the sports that they were involved in. Brian added that he was also fortunate to have his photograph taken with him. Meanwhile, he was training in readiness for the next big occasion, the National Championships, held at Sheffield. Besides training at Lodge Moor Sports Club, he also went to the gym at the local steelworks at Stocksbridge, Number 3 gate. 'Not modern,' Brian remarked, 'but no-one pushes you, you can train yourself. It's a good place, with good people.'

In 1979, Brian did extremely well in the National Championships. He came first, taking the gold medal with a personal best lift, of 408lbs (185 kilo's), 3 times his own body weight. This great event was followed by the 1980 Paralympics. They should have been held in Moscow, but because of political problems the venue was changed to Arnhem, Holland. Brian did not do as well in this event, coming fourth, but the outlook changed when the next Olympic meeting came around in 1984. The Paralympics were supposed to have been held in Champagne, Illinois, but again the venue was changed. This time to Buckinghamshire, England. The reason given, Brian stated, was that it was not financially viable to be held abroad. Still in the feather-weight class, Brian became the Olympic Champion, taking

Late 1980s, Brian talking to Princess Diana at Sheffield.

the gold medal. He remarked that it was the finest feeling in the world when he received it and the *National Anthem* was being played.

On 18 March 1985, he was requested to attend a reception held at 10 Downing Street. The invitation came from Mrs Thatcher, the Prime Minister, and her husband, Dennis. This was in honour of Brian Stones's achievements. 'It was a wonderful evening,' Brian smiled at the memory, 'there was Tessa Sanderson, Bob Monkhouse, and a host of famous celebrities.' The next stage in Brian's career was the Olympics in 1988, held in Seoul, South Korea. He went there to defend his title, but came fifth, losing to a competitor from Guatemala. Brian was weakened from de-hydration, and he only attempted two lifts. The highest was 157 kilo's, and the gold medal was won with 177 kilo's. As he said, and I fully agree, 'coming fifth in the world is no mean feat.' One of Brian's happiest memories of Seoul, was the Olympic flame being lit in front of a crowd of 70,000.

It was in the late eighties, that Brian was asked to take part in two different demonstrations of power-lifting at Sheffield. In the first one, he was introduced to Princess Diana. He found her to be an interesting person to talk to, and a down-to-earth character. They discussed keeping fit, and one of her ways was to go swimming every morning. Brian said that she just sat on the end of the bench, and they were bombarded with questions from BBC and Yorkshire Television crews. Brian hoped to get sponsorship for the disabled, because in his opinion it was sadly lacking in those days. When he spoke to Prince Charles, it was more formal. Brian spoke to him about playing polo, but he was not as forthcoming as his wife had been.

Sadly, Brian and Lynda went their separate ways and she re-married. He asked me to print a letter to her. Here it is:

After my accident, I owe it to my ex-wife, Lynda for assisting me in the early days in training, and recovering from my injuries. With her encouragement, patience, and putting up with me, it gave me the will to live. Otherwise, I would never have made it. She also gave me a beautiful daughter, which got me through a traumatic period of my life.

Brian also wishes me to add, that he was thankful to Keith Lodge of the *Barnsley Chronicle* for the excellent coverage that he has given him throughout thirteen years of a competitive sporting career.

These days, Brian still keeps himself fit. He trains, but doubts that he will compete at international level again. He is a proud man, and the gold medals that have come his way have been richly deserved.

24. CHARLIE WILLIAMS

Footballer and Star Comedian

WHO WOULD THINK THAT old-fashioned term of endearment, 'me old flower', would be immortalised into a catch-phrase. Charlie Williams, a man with a big smile and heart to match springs to mind. When I visited him at his home near Birdwell, it wasn't like meeting a stranger, because he used to be such a familiar face on television. Charlie's life began in 1927 when he was born in Royston, near Barnsley. His mother, 'Yorkshire bred and born', lived in Royston, her name was Doris. His father, born in the British West Indies, Barbados, was named Charles. I asked Charlie if I should address him during our chat as Mr Williams; his reply was, 'No me old love, there's only tax man that has right to do that'. Because Charles senior lived in a British Colony, he had to fight for Britain in the First World War. Later, he travelled around England, decided that there would be more opportunity here, and settled in Royston along with two cousins.

The family did not stay, moving to nearby South Hiendley, where Charlie attended the local schools, along with his little sister. 'Sadly', Charlie said, 'I lost her a couple of years ago with cancer'. The young Charlie was always playing football for his school team. 'Aye', Charlie remarked, 'I can remember the sports master as clear as day. He taught science as well, you know. His name was Gordon Mills,' Charlie pondered for a while, 'I can remember Mr Cartwright the Headmaster, Sam Mills the maths teacher, and Mrs Robinson who taught geography. I was happiest though, playing football'.

When Charlie was fourteen, he left school and started work down the mine at Monkton Colliery, near Ryhill. His father died when he was sixteen, so Charlie went to live with his relations, his uncle and his cousin at Upton. There he started at Upton Colliery, when he was then seventeen-and-a-half. He was still playing football, and to a good standard since at the age of nineteen, he signed professionally for Doncaster Rovers. The person who had encouraged him, his schoolmaster friend Don Gordon, used to go and watch him. Charlie mentioned that he too had died a couple of years previously, in his eighties, and was sadly missed.

Charlie's first professional match was in October, 1948. He made

The Doncaster Rovers Football Team, 1956/57.

his league 'debut' for the Rovers against Tranmere Rovers, at Belle Vue, in the last match of the 1949/50 season. The date was 3 May 1950, the result was 1-1. Reserve team football followed, before he next appeared in a first team match versus Plymouth Argyle. They played at home on 15 January 1955, the result being 3-2. The 1955/56 season saw him play in every first team fixture as well as scoring his only league goal for the club, against Barnsley, at Oakwell, 24 March 1956. The Rovers 'strip' was red and white, so whenever they played at Oakwell, they had to change colours. Charlie remained a regular member of the Rovers first team before playing his last league game at home to Bradford City, 22 November 1958. He played 158 league games for Doncaster, scoring one goal, and 16 FA Cup games. This gave a total of 174 first team games.

Charlie married in 1957, and for the last two years of his time with the Rovers, he lived in Doncaster, near the Infirmary. After leaving them, he signed for Skegness Football Club and lived there for the next three years. By this time, Charlie was in his early thirties and he decided to leave professional football. He and his wife came back to South Heindley, where he drove a lorry for a living. He still played football for a local team, Grimethorpe Miners' Welfare. Charlie particularly remembers playing alongside 'Skinner' Normanton, the great Barnsley footballer who too, was at the back end of his career. Charlie had two children, a boy and a girl to support so he had to look around for a change of employment. He started work for the National Coal Board, as a fitter at their Shafton workshops. To supplement his income, Charlie started to go around the working men's clubs as an entertainer. Mainly he sang, interspersing his act with a few jokes. The concert secretaries' told him that there was more money to be made as a comedian at that time, rather than singing. Charlie laughed, 'Being a Yorkshireman, I thought, 'Aye, Aye, I'm having a bite at this'. So it became, 'Charlie Williams, comedian'.

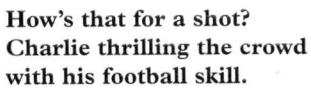

How's that for a shot? Charlie thrilling the crowd with his football skill.

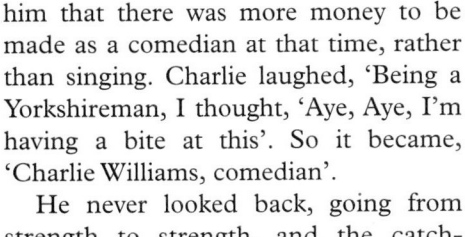

He never looked back, going from strength to strength, and the catch-phrase, *'me old flower'* was born. He signed up as a full-time professional stage artist in 1970. In 1972, Johnny Hamp, a producer and director, asked Charlie and a few more entertainers, amongst them, Duggie Brown and Colin Crompton, if they would do a pilot show called *The Comedians* for television. This took place in the Manchester studios. The initial showing was an instant success, and it became a weekly series, a showcase for Northern talent.

In 1974, Charlie was offered the job of hosting *Golden Shot.* This was a television game show, made famous by Jackie Rae and other stars. Many readers will remember that it involved aiming at a target with a crossbow with a television camera mounted on it. A viewer at home gave directions via the telephone instructing Bernie the cameraman to align the crossbow with the target. This gave birth to another catch-phrase,

Bernie- the Bolt! Charlie was a household name by now, and he and his fellow comedians were in great demand. He signed for the new show for a period of six months, with an option of twelve but realised after four months, that he had bitten off more than he could chew. He was already booked for fourteen months in advance with other commitments, working six days a week. This extra show meant that he also had to travel to Birmingham every Sunday. It proved to be too much, and after four months, Charlie resigned. As he said, 'To experience it, you had to take part in it'.

Charlie is grateful that he has been able to make his way in the world. He spoke about the past again, when he was a miner. His first wage packet was £1.13s. Whilst he was at Upton Colliery in 1953, working on the haulage, his weekly wage was £8-15s. It was there that he received the letter asking him to join Doncaster Rovers where the money was £10 per week, playing in the reserves. After he signed, it quickly went up to £14, and then £17. As Charlie said, 'Still better than the average working man in those days'. He added that miners earned every penny.

Charlie purchased his present home in 1973, moving in after renovations in 1974. Sadly, his marriage was to end and he spent two years on his own. He met Janice, his present partner, in 1984. They married on 28 March 1992. Janice is a friendly lady, we sat in the conservatory on a pleasant afternoon, with the sun streaming through the windows. Charlie is frailer now, suffering from arthritis, but that same cheerful grin is still there. We chatted on and discussed quite a few things, ranging from smoking to Portsmouth footballers. He retired in December, on his 68th birthday. What he didn't tell me was of his involvement with the disabled, such as helping out with charitable events. Charlie has got the unique ability of being able to make people laugh, a talent to cherish in life. He has also had the skill needed to sustain a football career. In the autumn of his years, he deserves good health, strength, and happiness.

25. TOMMY TAYLOR

Barnsley, Manchester United and England Footballer

(As told by his friend Harry England)

TOMMY TAYLOR is a Barnsley footballing legend. A man who became his best friend, Harry England, recounted this story to me. They both lived in the Smithies area of Barnsley and went to school together. Tommy was born on 29 January 1932, to parents Charlie and Violet. He had three brothers, Bill, Alec and Albert, and two sisters, Irene and Alice. The house that he was brought up in ran alongside a path at the back of the *Woodman Inn,* Wakefield Road, number 4 Quarry Street. It was in the fields around this area, Rotherham Road, and the back of the *Athersley Arms* pub, that Tommy, Harry and their mates used to kick a ball around. They used to swap football photos and practically live in each other's houses. 'This resulted,' as Harry recollected, 'in them being lifelong bosom pals.' One story that Harry related was about breaking someone's kitchen window with the football. The tenants of the house were away, so in the end the boys clubbed together for a new window. They carefully stretched an arm through the gaping hole and left the money on the sill. Harry chuckled, 'Our consciences were appeased that way.' Tommy's family had by then moved house, the new address was 4 St Helen's Avenue, Smithies. The year, 1941. His elder brother Billy signed as an amateur at Oakwell as a centre-forward when he was sixteen. Harry said that he was a good player in his youth but did not extend his career.

Tommy played football for Raley Secondary Modern School and Barnsley Boys, graduating to Smithies United in 1948. After leaving school, he worked on the pit-top at Wharncliffe Woodmoor 1, 2 and 3. He was running his football career alongside his work. This carried on for two years and eventually Tommy's talent was noticed and on 6 February 1948 he was signed up by Barnsley Football Club, for the princely sum (as Harry narrated), of ten pounds. This was as an amateur. He quickly made his way through the ranks and signed professionally on 25 July 1949. His First team debut was against St Mirren for the Paisley Charity Cup on 2 May 1949. However, Tommy received his calling-up papers for National Service, and he

Harry England ***(left)*** **with Tommy in their younger days.**

went into the Forces on 25 May 1950. He was posted to Tonfirnan, Merionethshire, in Wales. This was not the end of his career, because he played for his Regimental team in Division One of the Welsh League. Also, for the Northern Command, playing with and against, many professional fellow footballers, who were also completing their time in the army. It was during this time, Harry said, that Tommy blossomed out into a mature man, taller, and of a stockier build. He also won medals as a sprinter and long-jumper.

Upon Tommy's return to Civvy Street, he resumed full-time footballing with Barnsley FC. He quickly resumed his outstanding performances which automatically resulted in clubs outside the area taking a keen interest in him, amongst them, Manchester United. His skill was brought to the notice of Matt Busby the manager, who put in a bid for Tommy Taylor. Joe Richards, the Barnsley Club Chairman shook hands with Mr Busby and the transfer fee was clinched at £29,999, a club record. Tommy wasn't particular happy at leaving Barnsley, the place where his roots were, but he signed on 4 March 1953, and the deal was made.The last League game that Tommy played for Barnsley was on 14 February 1953, against Lincoln City. In all, he appeared 46 times for his home town, scoring 28 goals in the process.

The next step was Old Trafford. Matt Busby was collecting a team of young men, the pick of the crop, for his dream of top football league players, amongst them, centre-forward Tommy and centre-half Mark Jones, also from Barnsley. The team became known as 'The Busby Babes.' Harry mentioned that when Tommy went to Manchester, he never forgot his old friends. He'd send cards and photographs from all over the world, wherever the team happened to be playing. Harry saved everything and has lots of memorabilia. I

Barnsley football team, 1952/53. From left to right *Back row:* **Jarman, Smith, Betts, Hough, Seed (Manager), May, Dougle, Shotton (Trainer).** *Front row:* **Kay, Chapple, Taylor, McMorran, Kelly, McNeil.**

asked him if he had tried to get anywhere with his footballing prowess when he was younger. Harry replied that he would have liked to, but he suffered from a broken knee-cap when he was twelve, thus putting paid to any chance of a football career. He had a brother, Alf England who showed promise. He played for Yorkshire Boys and was chosen to appear for England. Another sad mishap came about for the brothers when Alf broke his arm, and so the England appearance didn't take place. He was snapped up by Wolverhampton however, when he left Raley school at 14. With the outbreak of war, Alf worked

Tommy chatting to his friends. Left to right, Frank Swift, David Pegg, Tommy Taylor, Mark Jones.

on the railway, classed as essential works during the war years. Afterwards, he worked as a football talent scout for Brian Clough and Peter Taylor in the Derbyshire and Nottinghamshire areas. He did not further his career any more.

Tommy Taylor made his Manchester United Football League debut on 7 March 1953, playing against Preston North End. His first FA Cup Game was on 9 January 1954, against Burnley, and his first European Cup Game for United was against Anderlecht on the 12 September 1956. He was a superb player and proved to be a very wise choice on the part of Matt Busby. Tommy's career was coasting along fine until the fateful day, Thursday, 6 February 1958. Manchester United had been playing Red Star at Belgrade the previous day in a European Cup match. The plane touched down at Munich in order to re-fuel. The passengers got off to go to the terminal building for a breather. Snow was gently falling and when everyone had returned to their seats the plane tried to take off. On the third attempt the plane started moving down the runway. The attempt was not successful and the aircraft broke in two. Eight Manchester United footballers died, amongst them being the two Barnsley men, Tommy and Mark. Others were Duncan Edwards, Geoff Bent, Roger Byrne, Liam Whelan, David Pegg and Eddie Colman.

Numerous reporters and officials did not survive either. Matt Busby, seriously injured, was taken along with other survivors to the *Rechts der Isar* hospital in Munich, where they began their battle for life.

Harry England could clearly remember the day that catastrophe fell. He said that he was just coming out of North Gawber pit, after working as a borer on the 10am shift. It was about 5 o'clock in the afternoon, Harry learned afterwards that it had happened two to three hours earlier. After the initial shock, he travelled to Old Trafford the following morning along with Billy Taylor, Eric Hodgson and Bob McCormick. Eric and Billy went into an office to find out what they could from officials. Harry said that they were hoping and praying that things were not as bad as had been reported, and Billy was living in the vain hope that his brother would be alive. This was not to be of course, and the City of Manchester fans sank into deep mourning. Indeed, it was a great shock throughout England. Matt Busby recovered, took up his position as manager again and was awarded the CBE, and eventually a Knighthood.

Tommy was buried amid great sadness in Monk Bretton Cemetery. His parents, who had cheered him on the sidelines, and encouraged him in every way, now share the same grave. Throughout Tommy's career with Manchester United, he played in 189 games, scoring 128 goals, and in 19 Full International Games he scored 16 goals. Not bad for the lad from Barnsley who had such a short career.

Tommy's United blazer which was given to Harry, now resides at Old Trafford in their museum, a fitting place for it to be. I asked Mr England to sum up. 'Tommy Taylor? He always had a smile, everybody thought the world of him. He never got a swollen head, and he never forgot his origins. A good mate.'

26. MARK JONES

Manchester United Footballer

(As told by his brother Amos)

MARK JONES was part of a family of six children, the other members being Tommy, Amos, Mary, Hilda and Irene. In the early years they lived at 21 Elliott Terrace, New Scarboro', Wombwell, with their parents Amos and Lucy. Mark was born on 15 June 1933, 'three years younger than myself,' Amos recounted. The children went to school at Darfield and then on to Foulstone Modern. This was then a new school. Amos said that he helped to prepare the sportsfield in readiness for future pupils, his brother Mark being one of them. The only place up until then that he and his brothers practised on was a football ground off Station Road, Wombwell. Amos their father had never played, but he bought the boys a proper case-ball, a luxury for some families in those days. Tommy, the eldest, was the first one to show promise. He finished up playing for Bradford City, but a leg injury sustained down the mine succeeded in curtailing his career twelve months afterwards.

As a boy, Amos recalled Mark being very keen when it came to kicking a ball about. One of the schoolteachers, Bill Payne, helped and encouraged him to further his talent. Mark played in the Don and Dearne schoolboys' football team, playing for England four times and gaining a cap in each instance. 'I can remember', Amos smiled, 'when mother used to go and watch him. In those days, he was already a big lad, fourteen years old and six foot tall, spectators were remarking on his size and they asked her jokingly if she was sure that it wasn't her husband that she had brought.'

It was here that Mark was spotted by Manchester United and quickly signed up. He had been training as an apprentice-bricklayer at the time. It was also at this time that he met his future wife, June. She worked at a baker's shop, and he used to call on his way from work. Centre-half Mark was the youngest ever player at sixteen to play in the United Reserve Team, quite a feat. He made his league debut for Manchester United on 7 October 1950, playing against Sheffield Wednesday at Old Trafford. Mark only made a few first team appearances over the next few years, but this changed on 10 March 1955, when he took Allenby Chilton's place against Cardiff.

Mark as a youngster. From left to right, Hilda holding Irene, Amos, Tom, Mark, Mary standing at the back.

Season 1955-56 saw Mark play in 42 games and achieve a First Division Championship Medal. One of his ambitions was to play in a Cup Final. This could have been achieved but for injuries sustained against Bournemouth the season after. Jackie Blanchflower took his place and succeeded in being chosen for the 1957 Cup Final. Ironically, Blanchflower was injured in December, not long after the start of the 1957/58 season, and Mark Jones was re-instated.

He had been playing in great style when his tragic and unforeseen death came about on 6 February 1958. The 'Busby Babes' and their manager, Sir Matt Busby were travelling from Munich by air when their plane crashed on take-off. Mark and another Barnsley man, Tommy Taylor perished in the disaster. One of the survivors was Sir Matt himself who overcame serious injuries. It was a tragedy that shocked the entire nation. Amos remarked that at first it was thought to be pilot error, but eventually it was decided that ice on the wings of the aircraft was to blame.

I asked Amos how it had affected his own family that day. He replied that three months previously their mother had died aged sixty. The day that Mark was killed was his mother's birthday. His father decided to go to work at the pit to try and take his mind off the loss of his wife. He was doing the afternoon shift when he was informed of his son's death. It was a crushing blow and one from which the family took a long time to recover. Mark's sister Irene, should have married when her mother passed away so she cancelled the ceremony. A new date was arranged, but it turned out to be the first Saturday after the death of her brother. After much persuasion she went ahead, but as Amos admitted, the wedding was tinged with sadness. Three of the couples in the family were expecting a child. Amos said that they all agreed that the first boy to arrive would be called Mark, after his late uncle. The first was to Pearl and Amos, and their elder son is indeed named Mark Jones, a television producer and director now living in Manchester, the place where his namesake resided. Amos and Pearl have two more grown-up children, John and Anne Elizabeth.

June and Mark Jones had two children, Gary who was two when

Portrait of the Jones family in their early years. From left to right, *Back row:* **Mark, Tom, Amos.** *Front row:* **Irene, Mary, Hilda.**

his father was killed, and Lynne born four months afterwards. In later years Gary might have travelled in his father's footsteps, but a broken leg put paid to that. I asked Amos if his brother had bothered with any hobbies when he was younger. 'Yes', he replied, 'he enjoyed walking his dog and breeding birds, mainly finches and budgies.' Amos described Mark's love of the gentle life, away from the cut-and-thrust of the competitive world of football. Everyone who came into contact with him, liked him. Pearl who was listening to the conversation said that so many people flocked to Mark's funeral, that the main gates of Wombwell Cemetary had to be opened for the cortege to pass through. The only time apparently that this had happened before was when Roy Kilner, Wombwell's famous cricketer was buried there. Normally, people used the side gate.

Stanley Fretwell, an old school chum of Mark's, and now a TV aerial erector, related an incident that happened in the classroom when they were children. The teacher, Mr Huntley, was taking the maths lesson. Stanley, sitting behind Mark and being extremely bored, started to torment him by tickling his neck. Mark swung his arm out, Stanley ducked, banged his head on the chair and finished up with a 'cauliflower' ear. But as he recalled, 'Mark was a smashing lad, a gentle giant'.

Amos chuckled when I recounted this story to him. 'Reminds me of the time when me and our Mark went to the kids' matinee at the pictures. It was a cowboy and indian film, and on the way home, he crept up behind me and pretended to cosh me with his toy gun. Unfortunately, it had a metal handle and my head was split open.' Amos touched his scalp ruefully, 'I will say this though, Mark was mortified and couldn't do enough afterwards.'

'Had Amos had a sporting career?' I asked. He replied that he had been very good at running. He had entered the 220 yards race in the Yorkshire Championships at Bradford in 1951, coming third. Also, when he was in the Police Force, he ran for the West Riding. Amos was a 'bobby' on the beat at West Melton, Liversedge, Stocksbridge and Worsbrough. Talking of 'flatfeet', he said that Mark had once given him a pair of brogues that he no longer needed. Because Amos was fresh out of the army at that time he believed in 'spit and polish'. He took the shoes to be soled and heeled, but when Mark saw them, he said, 'Hey, I'll have those back.' Amos smiled at the memory, 'That's brothers for you.'

Even though Mark Jones died forty years ago, he is still very much alive in the thoughts of his family. They are very proud of him, and rightly so.

27. ERIC WINSTANLEY

Barnsley Footballer and Coach

ERIC WINSTANLEY, football star of the 1960s and 1970s originated from Cundy Cross, Barnsley, son of Alexander and Florence. He was born on 15 November 1944. As a child, Eric went to Hoyle Mill School, Pontefract Road, Barnsley, but when a new housing scheme came into being at Athersley North, the family settled down there. Eric was ten years old at the time, and went to St Edwin's Junior Boys' School. After taking the eleven plus exam, he was sent to Longcar Central Senior School where he stayed until he was aged fifteen. Eric had fond memories of his time spent there. In particular he enjoyed the woodwork lessons that Mr England taught. I agreed with him that it was a very fine school, because I went there for a short while, they were happy days and the teachers were hardworking.

Eric excelled in all kind of sport from a very early age. When the family were living at Cundy Cross, he remembers his brother-in-law, who was married to his eldest sister, carrying him on his shoulders to Oakwell when great players such as Johnny Kelly were playing for Barnsley. Young Eric was fascinated. Coming from a large family (he has four sisters and a brother) meant that he was never short of help and encouragement. The whole family were keen on football. His father, brother, and uncle played. Brother Ralph, played for his school until he went in the R.A.F. 'Uncle' Ernie Hine, was really Eric's father's cousin, but Eric was brought up to call him uncle. Ernie played for Barnsley from 1921 to 1926, leaving for Manchester United and Leicester City, then rejoining from 1934 to 1938. He also played internationally, and was a record goal scorer for Barnsley. Both he and Alex encouraged Eric in every way.

From the age of seven Eric played football for whichever school he attended, usually as an inside-forward and was thrilled whenever he scored a goal. He played for Barnsley Boys up until the age of fifteen, when they were struggling for a centre-half, so this was the position bestowed upon him at this early stage of his career. From fifteen to seventeen, Eric was an apprentice-professional. This meant that although he worked with the ground staff at Oakwell, he could also play football. This was a way of becoming a professional footballer. Eric explained that nowadays there is a School of

Eric leaping to the ball at Villa Park.

Excellence for youngsters, and they also play in local Sunday League's, but in his day it was mainly left up to teachers to promote any youngster with talent. 'The teachers', Eric continued, 'were willing participants and very happy to use their coaching abilities after school hours. This is no longer as common, the youngsters now play more local Sunday football.'

When Eric moved to Athersley North, he can remember the sports teacher at his school saying, 'I understand you play football, Winstanley, so you can play tonight after school'. This message had been passed on from Eric's previous school at Hoyle Mill. This pleased young Eric, because apart from being able to play his beloved sport, it also meant that he could miss a couple of lessons when he had to play away during school hours.

When Eric signed at fifteen to work on the ground staff, the manager at that time was Johnny Steele, and his assistant was Norman Rimmington. Eric said that it gave him a brilliant feeling, to know that he was involved with Oakwell. He mentioned that it was a lot better for youngsters then because they did not have the same pressure. If football did not work out, there were lots of other vacancies in the mines or factories, unlike today. Eric was thrilled with his first wage packet in 1960 when he was fifteen. It was £4, with stoppages £3.12s (£3.60p) to take home to mum. In the summer of 1962, came every young lad's dream, he was offered a contract. He signed as a professional for the 'Reds' and played in the reserve team.

Eric Winstanley can clearly remember his first team debut. He was selected to play for England Youth at Swindon. Whilst staying at the hotel on the Friday night he received a phone call saying that centre-half Duncan Sharpe had been injured, and he was to take his place. The match was against Brentford, in London. The following day, Eric donned the number five shirt and gave of his best. The score was 1-1, not a great game, but an occasion for Eric to remember. There was a further match with Queen's Park Rangers a few days later, but the following weekend, Duncan Sharpe was fit again and Eric had to take his place in the reserves once more, but he'd had his introduction to first-team football. At the end of the season, he was picked to play for England in the Youth World Cup tournament in Rumania. Billy Wright was team manager. England Youth played three matches. When Eric returned to the club, in the summer of 1962, Duncan Sharpe announced his retirement from football. He was a hard act to follow, but Eric was offered a regular position of centre-half, thereby fulfilling his dream.

Eric Winstanley played two full seasons and was made team captain when he was only nineteen, a remarkable achievement. Unfortunately, he missed half the season, plus the whole of the next because of a bad knee injury. It was his left knee, and Eric being a left-footer, wondered how he would fare. He had an operation at Barnsley General Hospital, Mr Evan Price being the surgeon. It was a complete success, and Eric played top-class football for a further thirteen years. He was very grateful to Mr Price, in Eric's words, 'That man saved my career'.

In 1968 Eric went with the Football Association representative team to Zambia to play some matches and to coach at the same time. Also in the team were future England manager Graham Taylor, and future Tottenham Hotspur manager Keith Burkinshaw. I asked him if they had trained anyone of any significance. Eric replied that they had. One of the young lads, Akim Masenga, became a national footballing hero in later years. Eric said that he was only a schoolboy at the time, but he was brilliant, and stood out from the rest. He too now has a coaching job in Africa.

Eric left the Barnsley FC in 1973, holding the record for the most league appearances. In all, he played in 460 games. He was transferred to Chesterfield as a centre-half, making it to Club Captain, and staying for four years. In 1977 Eric's knee started to play up and he decided to retire. He was offered a job coaching the Navy Team in Zanzibar, East Africa. He said that it was a lovely tropical island and the football was good. In one way Eric said that it reminded him of his own youth, there was so much raw enthusiasm. 'You had to rough it sometimes', he recollected, 'being a Third World Country, but it was a marvellous experience'.

Eric in action.

By now Eric had two boys of his own, Mark and Andrew. He and his wife, Margaret, had married in 1970. Whilst Eric was at Zanzibar, the boys flew over in the six weeks' summer holidays, to be with him. Whilst they were there, cholera broke out. This proved to be a particularly worrying time and the flight back home was delayed because of this. After fifteen months' coaching, Eric was offered a three year contract along with a lovely house on the coast. He was having a wonderful time with football training on the beaches and surveying the untapped talent of the young recruits. Eric travelled to Uganda, Ethiopia, Somalia and Tanzania. They were all competing for the Eastern Central Club Championship. At a function by the side of Lake Victoria, Eric met Idi Amin. Whilst there fighting broke out between Uganda and Tanzania. The only way out - to go back to Tanzania - was on Idi Amin's private plane, an army plane designed like a carrier, with seats down the middle. On his return to Tanzania, Eric was kicking his heels for the next few months. He was in charge of the Navy team, and they and the Army, Police and Aerial teams were fighting the war. All football was suspended, and Eric was extremely disappointed because he and they, had enjoyed it so much. He came back to England during the bad winter of 1979.

Eric bought a General Dealer's shop in Monk Bretton which his wife still runs today. Johnny Steele got in touch with Eric and asked him if he would like to assist with the commercial side of the business at Oakwell, involving promotions, lotteries, etc. Eric agreed, and helped the late Brian Hanley, who was then Commercial Manager, along with Team Manager Alan Clarke. They were doing very well at the time. However, when Norman Hunter took over, he asked Eric to transfer to the coaching and scouting side. Eric accepted, it was more in his line of work. This was the season 1981/82. Since then, and to this present day, he has remained on the coaching staff, and having worked under six different managers.

I asked Eric which was his proudest moment. He replied that it was when Barnsley played Manchester United, and he was up against such greats as George Best, Dennis Law and Bobby Charlton. This was in 1963, in front of a crowd of 38,076. They were beaten, but it was a great experience. Eric's all-time personal Barnsley favourite was winger Arthur Kaye, ('Mr Magic'), the best player he had ever seen playing at Oakwell.

Summing up, Eric gave his views of football as a career for today's youngsters: 'In my youth, when we came home from school, I wanted to be outside all of the time, kicking a ball about. Today, there are many other distractions, for example, computers. Natural sporting abilities are being squashed. But for the youngster with dedication there are opportunities out there'.

28. NORMAN RIMMINGTON

Footballer and Coach

NORMAN RIMMINGTON has had a long career in the footballing world. He was born in Mapplewell, to parents, Harry and Florence on 29 November 1923. As a youngster, Norman went to the local Infant and Junior schools, finishing up at Darton Senior. It was during his schooldays that playing a game of cricket or football was most important to him. He was a 'natural', at both games. Norman's father did not encourage him too much, because he thought that education came first and would afford him a better living as an adult than a sporting career. Unfortunately, Harry died when Norman was sixteen, so he was not around to see his son make a success of his life.

Norman left school at the age of fourteen and started work underground at North Gawber Colliery. During this time, he was still playing football for his local team, Barugh Green. He can remember earning twelve shillings and sixpence (72.5p) for six days work at the pit. Ernest Plant spotted Norman playing football when he was then playing with Towncroft Working Men's Club at Mapplewell. Ernest was a football scout, and the result of this encounter led to Norman being offered a trial for Barnsley Football Club. This was just before the war finished, in 1944. Norman signed and trained alongside such players as Roy Cooling, George Robledo, Lewis Clayton and Jack Harston. These men had all worked down the mines too. During the war years, mining was classed as an essential occupation, so miners could not join the forces. Norman volunteered for the RAF but was not allowed in. He said that signing at Oakwell was nothing elaborate in those days. It was in 1944, that Norman married Jessie. He still worked down the mine, because even when the war ended in 1945, he could then have been called up for two years' National Service. It was in his interest to stay in Barnsley then, at the start of a flourishing football career.

I asked Norman if he had always played in goal and why. He replied with a chuckle that if you were a bit of a big lad at school, then more often than not, the teacher would select you as the 'goalie'. Norman enjoyed this position so much that he decided to make it his own. His first match for the First Team was in 1945/46 playing away at Huddersfield. Cliff Binns, who should have been the

Taken in December, 1967. Norman as trainer for Barnsley FC.

goalkeeper was injured, so Norman was called upon as a replacement. It was a thrilling game for him, and memorable too. In Norman's words, 'There was a hell of a crowd there, you know'. Because the fixture came shortly after the war years, Norman mentioned that the game was for the 'Victory in Europe Cup'.

The first match that Norman was chosen for his 'debut' proper, was at Coventry when Barnsley were in the old second Division. It was the season of 1946/47 and both sides drew, 2-2. Another match that Norman remembers with pride was again at Huddersfield, the same season, in the third round of the FA Cup where nearly 40,000 attended, taking £4,994 at the gate. The team was Rimmington, Pallister, Wilson, Cunningham, Bennett, Smith, Glover, Kelly, Baxter, Robledo and Asquith. The result was a resounding 4-3 in favour of the Reds, a great start for Norman. In those days there was a lot of competition at Oakwell, with five goalkeepers and around forty other professional players. After being with the club for one season, and a small part of the following, Norman sustained an injury to his shoulder-blade, dislocating it. He was playing in the reserves at the time. It resulted in him being off for thirteen weeks, and eventually in 1947/48 he was transferred to Hartlepool, Pat Kelly taking his place with Barnsley, followed by Harry Hough. Norman stayed with his new team for the next five years, mentioning that nothing very notable happened.

On leaving Hartlepool, Norman played one season of non-league matches at Buxton, but retired at the age of thirty-two. He had suffered a few small fractures of fingers and toes. He said, 'It's remarkable, you can go for a clear season with no injuries, and then all of a sudden you get them in a row.' Norman was still working down the mine, and thinking perhaps that his involvement with Oakwell was over, when he was asked if he would coach the 'A'Team. At that time, Tim Ward was manager, and Bob Shotton trainer. I can clearly remember the night I was asked', Norman smiled, 'I was up a ladder doing some decorating at home'. He asked what the job entailed. He was to watch the players, assess them, and then send a written report in about their progress. Also to look after them, and to be in charge on match days. It was part-time work. Norman agreed. It was 1955 and by 1956, he had the joy of seeing them reach the final in the Yorkshire League Cup.

In 1960 Johnny Steele was appointed manager, and he asked Norman if he would also look after the juniors. He was happy to do this until 1962, when he became a full-time coach for the first team. He also obtained his Treatment for Sports Injuries Certificate. Norman coached until 1973 when the groundsman left. He applied for the post and was successful, remaining until 1978 when Alan Clarke asked him to serve as physiotherapist. This suited Norman admirably and he continued until retirement age. After this, Chairman Geoff Buckle asked him if he would help the groundsman and offer any advice needed which might be of advantage to the club. Again, Norman agreed and did the job for a while, but then Viv Anderson asked him to take care of the kit. Norman said that because of his age he would like to do it, and it has worked out quite well.

**Celebrating their promotion from Third Division to Second Division in 1981/82. From left to right:
Bobby Collins, Norman Rimmington, Ian Evans, Norman Hunter, Johnny Steele.**

Norman spoke about his family life. He has two daughters, Anne and Margaret, and four grandchildren. Although three of them are boys, they have not shown any desire to be footballers. This brought him to Eric Winstanley, who was present at the interview. 'I can remember Eric when he was a young lad', Norman went on, 'I saw him in his first game in the juniors. He played outside-left and scored. Brilliant. Since then, I have watched his progress throughout the years'.

In return, Eric added, 'Norman won't tell you this, but he has been of great value to me and to the club. Young managers have benefited from his help and experience, and it's good to have someone like him around'. Norman gave a modest reply, 'Well you've seen it all before, that way you can help, can't you?' Norman thinks that the Reds have a great future, saying that he can't believe his eyes at the reconstruction work that has taken place at Oakwell over the last three or four years. He continued, 'It's tremendous, the way the ground and seating has improved, the seats alone take just under 20,000'. He also mentioned 'Barnsley are on a level with any team in this area. At one time the players were all paid the same, and entry into the game was on a similar basis. However, circumstances are different now and if anyone was fortunate enough to make it to the Premier League, then they had it made'. There have been many changes, but Norman has seen his beloved Oakwell through the years, and hopefully with quite a few more to come.

29. MAURICE FIRTH AND BARNSLEY BOYS FOOTBALL

Maurice Firth. Barnsley FC Youth Liaison Officer, 1996.

MAURICE VERNON FIRTH, Barnsley Football Club's Youth Liaison Officer is highly knowledgeable when it comes to the history of Barnsley Boys Football. I asked him about his own life, and how he had become involved. Maurice was born on 8 July 1931 to Percy and Marion in the village of Dodworth, where he spent most of his life. His father is now aged 86, but his mother died when she was 59. He attended Keresforth Road School, Dodworth, at the age of three, staying there until eleven, then going on to Penistone Grammar School. Here he furthered his education until 1949, leaving for the army. In 1953, when military life was over, Maurice obtained a teaching post at Grove Street School, opposite the Oakwell football ground. Although he had played local football in earlier years, he was more interested in coaching.

Doncaster Road School defeated Eldon Street North School at Oakwell, 1921, winning the Barnsley Cup. A Greenoff, Berry Bridge *(England International)*, **W Smith, S Paynter, W Deakin, J Bellamy, P Whitehead, H Ibbotson** *(second, front row)*, **G Swallow, A Slater, H Hall, Mr A Collier, Mr F Fearnside (Headmaster).**

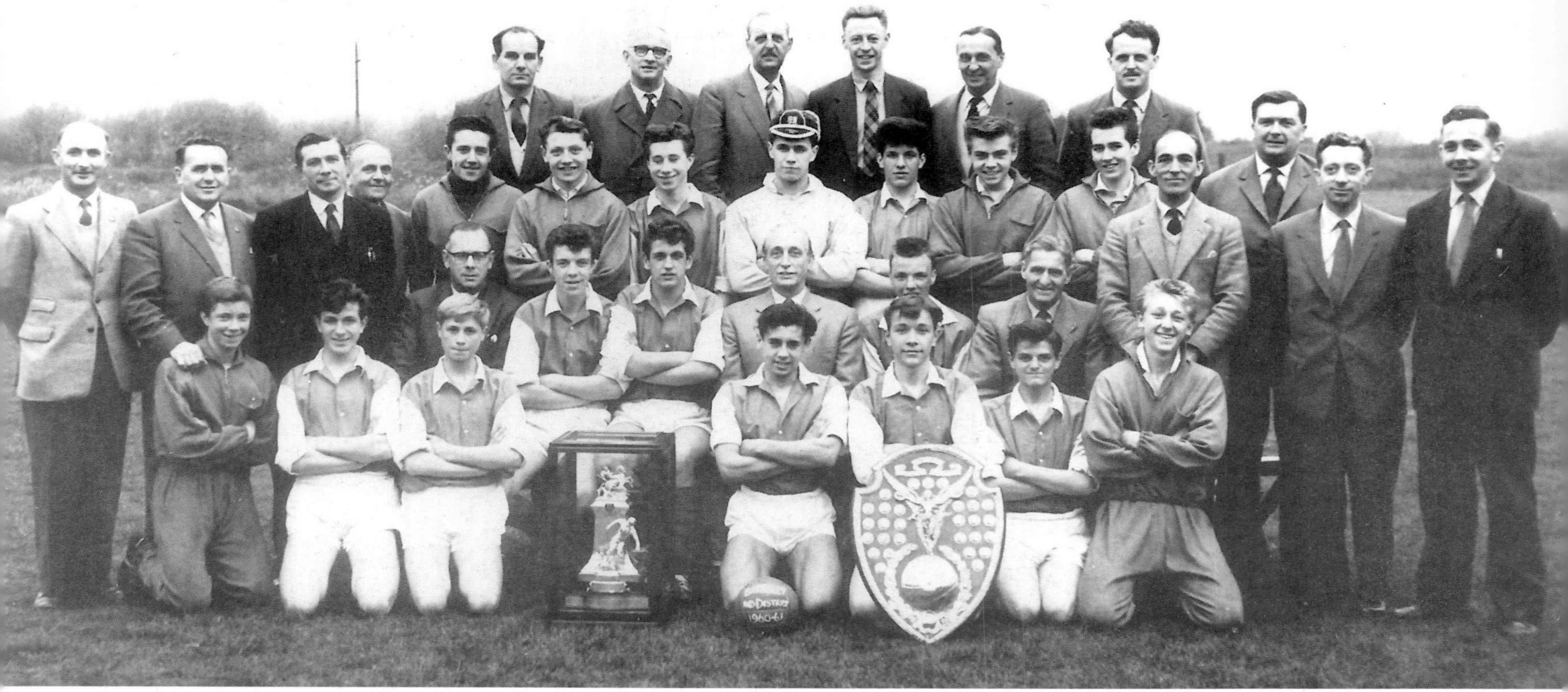

'Champions of England'. **This photograph of the highly successful Barnsley Boys team, reserves and officials was taken at the Dearne Ground on Thursday 18 May 1961. The Boys' team as follows:** *Back Row, left to right:* **Brian Elliott, Geoff Rushforth, Keith Marriott, Alan Ogley (wearing England Schoolboys cap), Ron Glover, Glen Duffield, Mick Mulligan.** *Middle Row (seated), left to right:* **Peter Farnsworth, Gordon Storr, Roy Gardner.** *Front Row (kneeling), left to right,* **Dennis Hutchinson, Alan Woodward, Jimmy Greenhoff, Howard Walker, David Kirk, John Hobson and Marshall. (Maurice Firth, on extreme right of the group.)**

'Boys Back in Town'. **The Barnsley Boys side of 1961 met up again for a special 'silver' celebration when most team members assembled at the Cross Inn, Royston in May 1986, twenty-five years after their English Trophy victory over Liverpool Boys. The meal was prepared by landlord Peter Farnsworth – identical to the one served up at the civic reception in Barnsley Town Hall. Only two players were unable to attend – Jimmy Greenhoff (ex-Leeds and Manchester United) who was coaching in Tenerife and Alan Woodward (ex-Sheffield United) who was living in the United States.**

Back row left to right: **Brian Elliott, Geoff Rushforth, Peter Farnsworth, Keith Marriott, Alan Ogley (wearing schoolboy international cap), Roy Gardner, Howard Walker (who had travelled from Canada), Glen Duffield and Mick Mulligan.** *Front Row left to right:* **Dennis Hutchinson, Gordon Storr, Ron Glover, David Kirk, John Hobson and Marshall.**

To join the Barnsley Boys Committee in the 1950s, was as Maurice quoted, 'Easier to break into the Bank of England.' Lots of people wished to serve on it, Maurice included. Two of the main priorities of entry, being time and effort. Clarry Hirst, the Head of Grove Street, was secretary around this time, and when Maurice took a vacant coaching job offered by Clarry, this qualified him for a place on the committee. The vacancy had been caused by Harold Rushforth leaving, a coach to Barnsley Boys for many years. They hadn't had much success before the Second World War, but in the post-war years, Ted Davies, Harold Rushworth, Fred Burton, and Clarry Hirst, banded together and tried to make a worthwhile team out of 'the boys.' This culminated in the Barnsley Boys winning the English Schools' Trophy and the Yorkshire Schools' Shield during the 1948/49 season. The Captain was Ron Archer.

In 1956, Maurice became Team Manager for the Barnsley Boys. It was part-time work, because he was still a schoolteacher. However, the team were a great success, and achieved the 'double' again during 1956/57, the captain this time being Barry Taylor. In 1959, a year before he left his teaching job at Grove Street, Maurice was asked to help with another team being started by Johnny Steele, Youth Team Manager, it was for the under-eighteen's in the local league. Maurice gladly accepted. In the early days, he remarked that the team used to be for fourteen to fifteens, and lads would give their right arm to be in it. There were trials, and they would finish up with a squad of sixteen for the year. Nowadays, they have teams of under 11, 12, 13, 14, and 15.

In 1960/61, the Barnsley Boys again won the English Schools' Trophy, the final being played at Anfield (Liverpool) and Oakwell. There was a gate of 23,000 spectators. The Captain was Gordon Storr. With these wins and money from the gates, the club was able to amass £5,000

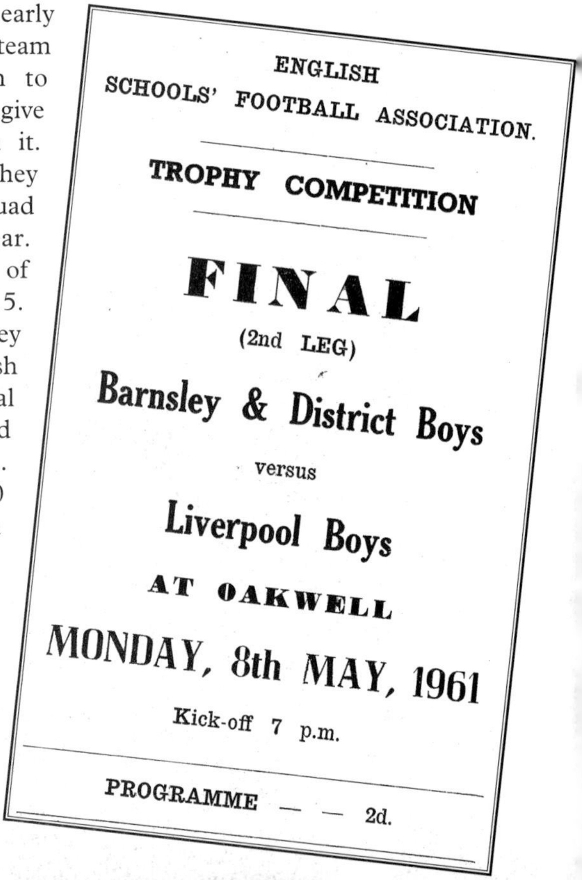
ENGLISH
SCHOOLS' FOOTBALL ASSOCIATION.

TROPHY COMPETITION

FINAL
(2nd LEG)

Barnsley & District Boys
versus
Liverpool Boys
AT OAKWELL
MONDAY, 8th MAY, 1961
Kick-off 7 p.m.

PROGRAMME — — 2d.

in the bank. They didn't touch the capital and lived off the interest. This was used for buying footballs, shirts, shorts, socks, etc. Meanwhile, Maurice's working life had led him to teaching at Kendray Junior School from 1960 to 1966. He then became Deputy Head at Worsbrough Common, and from there, Head of Wilthorpe Junior School. Retirement followed in 1991.

Before this however, the money in the bank was gradually whittled away over the years. Expenses were high, and finance for the teams has to be sharply scrutinised now. Maurice remarked that travelling expenses were high. If they got into the quarter-final, the semi-final, and the final itself, it could involve travelling all over England. The last time that the Barnsley Boys won the English Schoolboys' Trophy was in 1991. They have also won the Yorkshire Shield numerous times. Friendly matches very often take place at the Dorothy Hyman Stadium, but if they are successful in reaching the final of the English Trophy and it is a home match, then it always takes place at Oakwell.

Maurice has worked in various capacities for Barnsley Football Club. His jobs have included Youth Team Manager, Reserve Team Manager, Youth Development Officer, Assessor, Talent Scout, and Second Team Coach. He is now, as we have seen, the Youth Liaison Officer. He mentioned some of the famous players that have passed through the Barnsley Boys: Steve Daley, one of the first million pound footballers, who went to Wolves; Alan Woodward who played right-wing for Sheffield United; Jimmy Greenough, Leeds United, Manchester United, and Stoke; Brian Greenough, Manchester

Three of the Barnsley Boys Team, Duncan Richards, Shane Whitehurst, and Kevin O'Connor, pictured with their parents in 1996.

United; Alan Hill, former Assistant Manager of Nottingham Forest, and Alan Ogley, the best schoolboy goalkeeper that Maurice has seen. He added that the latter, having been transferred to Manchester City, would have gone on 'to great things,' but unfortunately, his eyesight handicapped him. Johnny Steele ranked Arthur Kaye as the best player ever to rise from the ranks of the Barnsley Boys. Maurice carried on, 'Eric Winstanley, the First Team Coach has done well too, and Phillip Chambers, who is now on the staff at Scarbrough Football Club. Also, there are lots of men who have done well in life, but didn't go into football.'

There was an interesting footnote to the match with Liverpool in 1961. One of the Barnsley players, Peter Farnsworth, was kicked in the mouth by an opposing player, Andy McCulloch, who later played for Sheffield Wednesday, Queen's Park Rangers, and Crystal Palace. Peter could not eat the celebratory meal held at Barnsley Town Hall because his mouth was swollen and he had several stitches in it. He couldn't even manage the soup. However, twenty-five years later, in 1986, Peter who was a publican by then, cooked an identical mouth-watering meal, and invited all the members of the former winning team to come and enjoy it. He also invited the coaches, Maurice and Eric Goddard. Peter at that time was landlord of the *Cross Inn* at Royston. He now runs the *Wilthorpe Hotel,* Huddersfield Road, and still has the public queuing for his delicious food.

Maurice Firth is married to Janet and they have two daughters, Julie in Australia, and who has two children herself, Elliott and Kate, and Clare who lives in Barnsley, with her daughters, Lauren and Bethany. Maurice Firth's life has centred around the Barnsley Boys for many years now. Hopefully, for a few youngsters, it will be the start of their success, in life as a whole.

30. ARTHUR K CLAYTON

Memories of Sporting Characters and Events

ARTHUR CLAYTON was born on 27 June 1901, to parents James Richard Clayton and Emily, (maiden name, Kay). The family lived at Hoyland Common and Arthur was one of four brothers, the others being Wilfred, Fred and Friend. I remarked that 'Friend' was a rather unusual first name, but Arthur said that it was in the family. He was thirteen when he left school, starting work at the same mine as his father, a pit deputy at Hoyland Silkstone Colliery. Arthur's first job was to pick the dirt out of the coal on the conveyor belt, a thankless task, but he enjoyed the comradeship of his workmates. After a spell at Hoyland Silkstone, he started at Rockingham Colliery and it was here that he stayed until his retirement at 65, forming a total of fifty-and-a-half years work underground, and eighteen months above ground.

Arthur spoke of his memories of Barnsley sportsmen. He could remember Charlie Hardcastle, the British feather-weight champion. Charlie used to visit a friend of his who lived on the same street as Arthur. 'He was always a smartly dressed young man' Arthur recalled. He went on to say that Charlie joined up between 1914/18 during the First World War. His last memory of him was as an elderly man working on the pit-top at Rockingham. Arthur said that you could see where boxing had left it's mark on him. Someone passed a remark that Charlie had not done very well out of boxing, but Arthur retaliated by saying that he'd been the top of his country in his profession, and that nobody else at the pit could say that!

When Arthur was a schoolboy, he recalled seeing a famous Mexborough boxer, 'Iron' Haigh in a boxing booth during Hoyland Common 'feast'. He also saw him in a film at the Miners' Institute fighting Sam Langford, an American. Unfortunately the Yorkshire-man lost, much to the locals disappointment.

Another hero in Arthur's eyes was a footballer, 'Tommy' Boyle. Born in Barnsley, but his family moving to Platts Common shortly after, Tommy began his footballing career as a member of the Hoyland Star Junior Club. The club folded after he had played a few matches with them, so he joined the Elsecar and Hoyland Town

Clubs. Whilst playing against Rockingham Colliery in 1904, he attracted the attention of Arthur Fairclough, Barnsley's Football manager. This resulted in him playing in the reserves in his first match for Barnsley, 30 September 1905. Eventually he became Captain and led his team in the FA Cup Final at Crystal Palace against Newcastle United in 1910. The result was a draw, 1-1. A re-play at Goodison Park resulted in disappointment for Barnsley, a 2-1 victory for their opponents. Tommy Boyle was transferred to Burnley on 30 September 1911, and six years to the day that he had made his debut for Barnsley Reserves. Tommy was crushed the year after when in 1912 the team that he had led earlier, won the English Cup Final under a different leadership. The game was against West Bromwich Albion at Crystal Palace. The final score was 0-0, so a re-play was arranged. This time the venue was at Bramall Lane, Sheffield.

An extract from the *Barnsley Chronicle* read at the time:

The conditions were ideal. Really the weather could not have been more favourable. It was uncomfortably hot for the spectators, and what the state of the players must have been in during a struggle which lasted 120 minutes, can well be imagined. Supporters of both clubs were greatly in evidence. The red and white of the Barnsley contingent predominated, but the pale blue and white colours of the West Bromwich Albion supporters showed that the Midlanders had a large following.

The score at half-time was 0-0. The second half remained the same

Barnsley's winning cup team, 1912 against West Bromwich Albion.

so further time was declared. in the last quarter, the *Chronicle* report ran:

Barnsley FC's mascot in the early 1900's.

On resuming, the Albion made a dash for the Barnsley goal but Downs was in the way and when the Yorkshire-men got going they were pulled up by Pennington. Bartrop made a weak effort, and West Bromwich gained a corner. This was of no advantage, and Barnsley were going great guns when they next invaded. Pearson only partially cleared a shot from Moore, and Bartrop shot in. Cook was in the way, and when Bratley shot, the leather again cannoned out of goal. It was the most exciting moment of the extra time, and how the Albion goal escaped is a mystery. The Midlanders responded with a corner, but the flag-kick was useless. A second corner fell to the Albion, and Cooper cleverly saved two smart efforts. He fisted away the flag-kick, and then cleared from Pailor. Glendenning called upon Pearson at the opposite end, and after a brief visit to the other end, Tufnell broke away on his own and getting quite clear of the backs, made no mistake. Pearson ran out, but Tufnell steadied himself and got the ball into the net amid a scene of tremendous excitement. West Bromwich made a desperate effort, and Shearman shot outside. It was all over, bar the shouting, for the remainder of play was in mid-field. When the whistle announced time, there was a memorable scene. The spectators rushed on to the field of play, and almost overwhelmed the Barnsley players. The finish was not without a sporting incident. Pennington, the Albion skipper and worthy International, rushed across to Taylor, and warmly shook hands with the Barnsley captain.

The result of this famous match was 1-0 in Barnsley's favour. Mr Clayton spoke of his memory of the Barnsley team's homecoming. He was only a young boy, but he can clearly remember standing by the roadside on the main Sheffield Road at Hoyland Common as the open charabanc made it's way from Sheffield to Barnsley. Everyone was in happy mood, the FA Cup being held aloft by Archie Taylor for everyone to see. It was a moment not to be forgotten, and has always lived on in Arthur's memory.

This was not the end for Tommy Boyle. Early in the 1913/14 season saw him play for England against Ireland. Also in 1914 he captained the Burnley team that won the FA Cup at Crystal Palace, which was the last final to be played on the Sydenham ground. The late King George V presented the trophy to Tommy. The 1914 to 1918 war saw him serving in the Royal Artillery on considerable active service. After the war, he helped Burnley to win the League Championship during 1920/21 when they played thirty consecutive games without a single defeat. Tommy Boyle died in 1940 whilst residing at Preston.

Arthur Clayton is a very interesting person to talk to. He is a softly -spoken gentleman with a wealth of memories and has achieved a great deal throughout his own life. At the age of 64, he started to teach local history to evening classes at Kirk Balk School where he continued until the age of eighty. His lectures were always carefully prepared and well-attended. He has written many articles, amongst them, The *Elsecar and Milton Ironworks,* and *A History of Earl Fitzwilliam's Elsecar Collieries*. He considers his best work to be *Parliamentary Enclosure*. In 1989, Arthur Clayton was honoured with a British Empire Medal. Now aged 96 and as alert as ever, he is a supreme example of lifelong learning.

Barnsley FC in the early years.

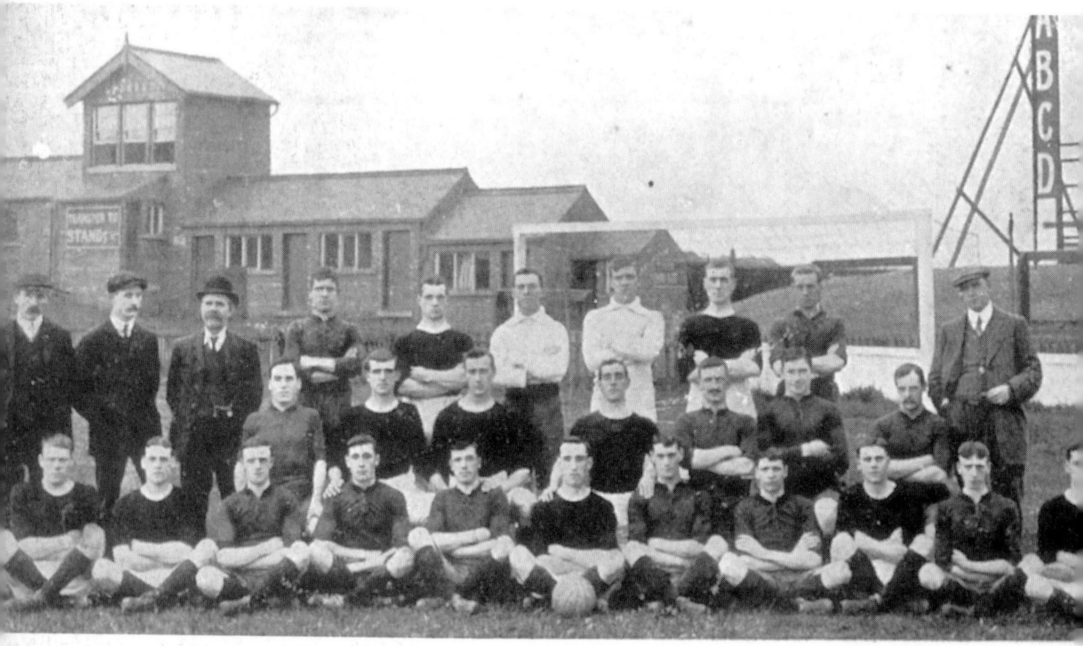

31. BARNSLEY LADIES FOOTBALL TEAMS

1918-1996

AN EXPECTANT hush fell over the ground. The player looked at the ball and seized the chance. One mighty kick and the ball soared over the half-way line and straight into the opposing team's goal-mouth! The third goal and the winner. The ground filled with the sound of the famous Oakwell roar. Had the 'Reds' scored? Was this the modern age of the nineties? I'm afraid not. This was 1918, and the teams were ladies. The captain of the match, and the scorer of the goals was my own grandma, Annie Barrett, my namesake. She was known to everyone as 'Nan'. They had battled their way to the final and it was for the Sugden Cup.

Grandma was in the Barnsley Shell Factory team of lady footballers and they were playing Templeborough NPF (Sheffield). It had been an exciting struggle in the presence of a large crowd of spectators at Oakwell. The teams were evenly matched and when time had been played the score was 2-2. An extra half hour was given and in the first quarter our Nan scored the aforementioned goal for Barnsley. The ladies worked at what used to be the Canister Company up Fitzwilliam Street. It was a munitions place during the First World War, and Grandma and Auntie Clara Hudson,her very best friend,worked there. They had both become widows during the war and had children to raise. My grandad, Walter Edward Barrett, had come home to convalesce after being wounded. He left grandma pregnant with her youngest child, his namesake, my Uncle Ned. He then went back to France and was killed on 22 April 1917.

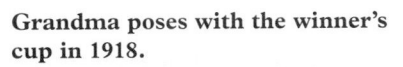

Grandma poses with the winner's cup in 1918.

I wrote a little about Nan in *Aspects of Barnsley 1,* about her trials and tribulations. She had five young children to care for, my dad Frank, Annie, Tom, Bessie, and Ned, and like lots of other young widows, precious little money to do it with.

Auntie Clara (I was brought up to

The shell factory football team, victorious Cup Winners in 1918.

call her auntie, out of respect) had two children, Jimmy and Tom. Both families were very close-knit, and spent a lot of time at each other's houses.

I first became aware of grandma being in a football team, when I read of her exploits in the *Barnsley Chronicle's* Fifty Years Ago column in 1968. It is only in recent years though that photographs of the team and the cup came into my possession. Some of these came from Uncle Tom, and some from as far away as South Africa, from my cousin Sonia, Uncle Ned's daughter. In conversation with Sonia's mother Audrey, she mentioned to me that Nan had once told her that King George, who was married to Queen Mary, was going to watch the match that I have just described. He had never seen a ladies' football team before, but there was a flu epidemic and the visit was cancelled, much to the team's disappointment.

I had always known that my grandma had a reputation of being a 'grafter'. Apparently, most people that knew her, marvelled at her strength. She could heave a sack of coal over her shoulders as good as any man. But for all her apparent toughness, she would give of her last. One of my very earliest memories in life was being held in her arms in her old rocking chair. I must have been extremely young to remember this, but a bond was formed between grandma and me which has never been broken. In later years, I rocked that old chair myself so hard that it sometimes tipped over and I banged my head on the mangle that used to be at the back of it. Can you remember the old washing machines that used to fold down? With a cloth draped over, it looked like another table.

It must have been particularly hard in the war years, for all the women whose husbands and sons were away fighting. For the men's part, I think that one of the most dreaded sentences for them to hear must have been the command, 'Men, over the top'. To climb out of the filthy, rain-soaked trenches and advance must have been heart-stopping. Knowing that it could be your last day on earth would also have been very daunting. They needed the women of course to keep the home fires burning, and to stage fund raising events such as ladies' football teams.

I have a possession of Grandad Barrett's, which fills me with wonder. It is his little notebook which he used as a diary throughout his travels in the First World War. He wrote of travelling through Egypt, and life in the trenches in France. When I think of the terrible deprivations that the soldiers had to live with, then I despair of the awful squalidness and pain that is brought about because of war. This diary, and some silk postcards are my legacy from him. I think I got to know him a little through these, my most treasured possessions. My brother Frank and cousin Sonia have his medals.

With hindsight, I wish many times that I had questioned grandma or my mother about these things, then it would have come from the horse's mouth so to speak. How many people doing the modern day thing of tracing their family tree, have berated themselves for not doing just that.

I must admit, when I saw the various photographs of the really early teams, it was amusing to see the football gear that was sported. I am

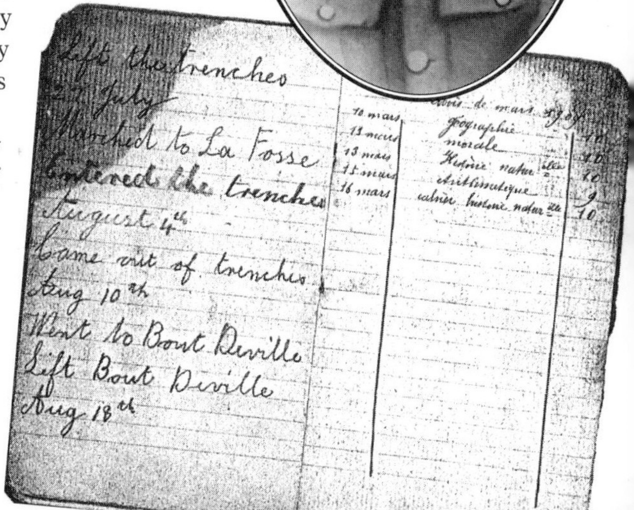

Left the trenches
27 July
Marched to La Fosse
Entered the trenches
August 4th
Came out of trenches
Aug 10th
Went to Bout Deville
Left Bout Deville
Aug 18th

A couple of pages out of grandad Barrett's diary

'Keep your hats on ladies.' The bobbin mill football team, photographed in 1918.

fairly sure that hats must have blown off in the wind, and with most women having long hair in those days, they must have had a problem. Headgear was dispensed with in later years, but around 1918 it was the done thing.

Whenever the ladies played, it was to help the war effort. Widows and orphans needed sustenance, and every penny raised was put to good use. I'm pretty sure that the ladies enjoyed it though. Nan and Auntie Clara threw their heart and soul into things, and both they and the team members would have felt well rewarded for their efforts.

To be truthful, I must admit to a strong sense of pride when I saw a picture of grandma with the cup. She would never have guessed that I would be sitting down and writing about it nearly eighty years on! A lady named Mrs Marion Bowman loaned me a photograph of the ladies who played for the Bobbin Mill, Pontefract Road, around the First World War years. Her father, Fred Hunter was a pattern maker under his own dad, Tom Hunter. This picture too had been passed down the family. 'Being an only child,' Marion told me, with a smile, 'I had to go to all the football matches with father'. This was much later than 1918, of course. In fact, Marion, being a singer and comedienne, was roped in along with lots of other entertainers to give concerts and raise funds yet again for the war effort. This was for the Second World War though, in the early forties. This was another facet of the British pulling together in times of strife.

Mrs Bowman toured the factories and clubs in this area, purely on a voluntary basis. She remembers going to entertain at a building which was on the site of what now is a supermarket in Worsbrough Dale. The Bass singer did not turn up because he had just had news that his son had been killed. Chatting to Marian, we realised that we ourselves had probably performed in the same show at Slazengers tennis ball factory. This was just after the war, but it was still for charity. I can remember my mother dressing me up as a gypsy. I danced around a make-believe camp-fire, and the cast sang Golden

Honeywell Ladies Football Team taken during the miners' strike in 1926. Left to right, *Back row:* **Florrie Townsend, Ivy Blackburn (Goalkeeper), Beatie Jakes, Mrs Townsend (Secretary).**
Middle row: **Annie Smith, Florrie Hurst, Lena Phillips (my auntie), Fanny Guest (mum's cousin).**
Front row: **Frances Phillips (mum), Florrie Jones, Gertie Jones, Mary Westwood, Annie Sapphire Phillips (mum's cousin).**

Earrings. So as you can see, entertaining, and football, helped to bring the money rolling in.

Besides factories and pubs, whole communities would become involved. The English love to stand around a field, be it any kind of weather and cheer their local team. Tactics and conditions are discussed at great length afterwards, and the individual merits of each player either praised or derided.

On the stroke of midnight, Tuesday, 4 May 1926, the General Strike began.British industries were paralysed as 4,000,000 walked out. This was another event in British history when people had to rally together and help each other in times of hardship. Yet again, Ladies' football teams were called upon to help the cause. My own mother, Frances Phillips, her sister Selena, and cousins, Fanny Guest and Annie Sapphire Phillips, all played for the Honeywell Ladies in 1926. Indeed, they won the last match of the season, by beating Monk Bretton Ladies for the Ladies' League championship. Their sporting gear was more modern than the 1918 strip. They wore neat, light coloured shirts and actually showed their knees, a step-up from earlier photographs. They had also dispensed with hats, favouring hair-nets, or in most cases, the 'bob'. This was a short hairstyle, very much in fashion, and I should imagine, a lot better for playing football in. During my research, I was sent a photograph of another team in 1926. Unfortunately, I could not thank the person concerned, because there was no name or address on the accompanying letter. However, the correspondent wrote that the picture was taken in Castlereigh Street, and it was the *Gardeners Arms*

Eagle ladies' football team, *Gardeners Arms.* **From left to right,**
Back row: **Leah England, Lily Turton, Florrie Powell, Annie Salveta.**
Middle row: **Florrie Barraclough, Unknown, Alice Reece.**
Front row: **Winnie Foy, Mary Hayes, Ethel ?, Madge ?, Unknown.**

team. They played under the name of 'Eagle Ladies'. They all looked quite cheerful and ready for business in their striped tops.

Moving up a few years to 1935/6 saw my father Frank Barrett, receiving a silver cup when he was captain of Kingstone United. They were runners-up in the B.A.F.U. SS League. Both he, my grandma, and my mother must have had a strong love of football.

During my research, I was introduced to a lady named Janet Houghton. She had played for the Shaw Inn Ladies who were based at Racecommon Road. A Mr Baxter had kindly loaned me a photograph of the team, because his wife had also played in it. Janet was able to give me the names of the team members, and a little bit of history. She was great friends of May, a lady who had married John Holden, the licensee of the *Shaw Inn.* In fact, she lived with them for many years. She too was a singer, and had many engagements at places such as the *Locke Inn, The Bush, Kingstone Club,* and the *Shaw Inn* itself. They used to play in a field at the back of the pub. In this field were some garages that belonged to Mr

1948. Shaw Inn Ladies' Football Team. From left to right,
Back row: **Alma Thornton, Joyce Chatterton, Jean Neal, Doreen Cooper, Vera Attleton, Dolly Jackman.**
Front row: **Janet Houghton, Josie Sanderson, Joan Stocks, Rae Armitage, Ruth Buckley.**

'Come on the Guide Posts'. A picture of the Wombwell based Ladies' Football Team taken in the late forties. From left to right; *Back row:* **Dorothy Sanderson, Pat Bedford, Phyllis Duke, Nora Auckland, Ethel Briggs, Lily Calvert.** *Front row:* **Mrs Harvey, Elsie Goulding, Mrs Siddons, Mrs Norburn, Kathleen Scott.**

Hyde, funeral director. The hearses were kept in them.

Apparently, the home team would have an advantage over the away team, because they knew every bump and hillock in the field. There was a distinct rise where everyone knew where to manoeuvre, except for the opposing side. They changed the name of the team to the Barnsley Ladies' Football Team, and played until 1951. They raised over £5,000 pounds for charity, and Marjorie Proops of the *Daily Mirror* came and interviewed them. She gave the team a good write-up in her column, which must have been a very proud moment for all concerned.

Another popular team around the 1940's, was the *Guide Post.* This was a pub based at Wombwell, on Brampton Road. Mr Sam Auckland, of Brampton, loaned me a photograph. His wife, Nora was one of the players, and they too raised a lot of money for the war effort and for charities. Mr Auckland has fond reminiscences of those early years. He can remember living at the lower side of the *Guide Post,* when the rent of their house was five shillings and threepence. He mentioned that a day's wage was five shillings and fourpence. He worked at Cortonwood colliery for 51 years. I asked Sam where the team used to play. He said that it was on a recreation field by the side of the 'Tracky' sheds at Wombwell. The committee organised the matches, but apart from the contribution by the ladies with their presence, they also made their own strip, and found their own football boots.

Over the years, ladies' football teams have proved to be a very valuable source of entertainment. But in the mid-fifties, the Star Paper Mill had a Ladies' Netball team. I was loaned a photograph of the team by Mrs Elva Gillott (nee Taylor) who was in the team herself, along with my cousin Mrs Maureen Walker, (nee Lowe). They played purely friendly matches, but it proves that team spirit is just as alive in women as it is in men!

Barnsley Ladies' Football Team is active and flourishing today. I have been in touch with a young woman, the team captain, Miss Joanne Vicary. Apparently the modern team stems from Lyons Bakery at Monk Bretton. It was formed in the summer of 1989. Tony Hannan, Head of Security at Lyons, came up with the idea of an all male football team to go to Hartlepool and play a friendly match. For a bit of inter-factory fun, it was suggested that a football team made up of ladies could accompany them and play another female team. They all travelled North, and the day was a huge success. With a great deal of pestering from Joanne, the team became permanent and the Lyons Cakes Ladies' Football Team was formed. The club is financially self-supporting, but does receive recognition from

Star Paper Mill Netball Team, 1954. From left to right; Audrey Barnes, Maureen Bywater, Doreen Frances, Maureen Lowe (my cousin), Elva Taylor.

Barnsley Football Club.

Women's football is far from being new to Lyons. As long ago as 1920, Lyons Mail reported that fifteen matches had taken place in January alone. This was only three years after the first serious football was played by women, according to the Women's Football Association.

Today, there are more than 400 teams affiliated to the women's football league. As previously mentioned, these matches were started because of charity. Lyons cake factory was responsible for sending sick children to Disneyland. They have also played at a summer fair organised to raise money for the Orphanage Appeal in Rumania.

The girls ran raffles to raise money to pay for their strip. Carlton Sports and Social Club also donated a sum of £455. This gave the team their red strip and their blue and yellow away strip. They all look good in these bright and cheerful colours. The team have been allowed to re-register with Women's F.A. under the name of Barnsley Ladies' Football Club. The head coach of the Community Football Programme, Alan Humphreys, also took over as manager, thus lightening the workload of Tony Hannan, who remained as Secretary. With Joanne as Captain, everything is set for a bright future. It is no flash-in-the-pan, because the women's FA Cup Final has been attended by over four thousand spectators. To end on a hopeful note, the latest football player in my family to step onto the hallowed turf of Oakwell, is one of my grandsons, Howard McFarlane. His parents are from Barnsley and Portsmouth, so he has played in both junior teams. Who knows, with a bit of luck, he might follow in his great, great grandmother's footsteps.

Lyons Cakes Ladies Football Team in their red and black 1995/96 kit. From left to right, *Back row:* **Donna Bradder, Lyn Wooding, Lisa McLoughlin, Gill Beaumont, Nicola Hearnshaw, Jo Smith, Jackie Millard, Tracy Allott.** *Front row:* **Geri Pursley, Tracy Smith, Michelle Herbert, Julie Camm, Joanne Vicary, Kerry Haynes, Louise Julian.**

32. 'GED' AND JOHN TUMMAN

Karate Experts

I INTERVIEWED GERALD TUMMAN and his son John, in their gymnasium at Regent Street South, Barnsley. Tucked away around the corner, and up a small alley, you could be forgiven for wondering what kind of place it could be, but it is quite surprising. After climbing the wooden stairs, the rooms are large and well-equipped. Framed photographs of teachers and pupils are dotted everywhere in various karate poses.

Gerald, or as everyone knows him, 'Ged', made us welcome, and we were introduced to his son John, who looked very muscular, hardly surprising, because he has done weight-training. Both father and son hold Black belts for karate. There was a certain amount of activity taking place in the gym, but we managed to find a quiet place and Ged began. Both his parents were Barnsley people, his father has passed away, but his mother is still living up Sheffield Road. Ged was born in 1938, and as a youngster he went to Blackburn Lane Infants' School (now the Polish Social Centre) and then on to the old Technical College. John, who was born in 1965, attended Longcar School, and then Barnsley Grammar.

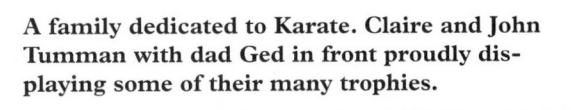

A family dedicated to Karate. Claire and John Tumman with dad Ged in front proudly displaying some of their many trophies.

Ged did not become interested in karate until 1972 when his son was aged seven. At that time he was working in the offices of the National Coal Board, first at Worsbrough Hall, and later at Grimethorpe. He did over thirty years with them. His son John, also worked for the NCB as an electrician, first at Dodworth, and then at Redbrook, until the pit closed. Besides John, Ged also had a daughter, Claire, aged four when he started his karate training.

Initially, Ged took John along to the Dorothy Hyman Stadium for him to be taught karate.

Because of John's tender age, he was told that he would have to stay and keep an eye on him during lessons. This inspired Ged to take part himself. He was already a keen sportsman, having enjoyed playing football. Eventually, Ged gained his Black belt, and with the help of Steve Swindle started his own club at Kingstone Parish Hall, Racecommon Road. This lasted from 1979 to 1988-9. Ged's daughter also became a Black belt during this time. In fact, both she and her brother have children themselves now, and they too are doing karate training. Very pleasurable for Ged and his wife Pat, to know that the whole family are interested in the sport.

Indeed, John says that for him, a fourth dan, and his father, a fifth, karate is a way of life now. The present gym was opened in 1989. They have around 120 pupils at this moment in time. The facilities are open every night in the week. John has won around three hundred trophies, travelling far and wide in the process. Besides competing all over England, he has been to Italy twice, Finland,

Demonstrating two styles of Karate kick. John; Mawashigeri. Ged; Maegeri.

Germany, and Ireland. In bouts abroad he has represented England. John modestly puts his wins down to luck, when in reality of course, it is just sheer hard work. Ged is still refereeing. Both he and John have retired from match fighting, but they still do karate every night, plus the training of their pupils. I asked them if it is mainly men that go to the classes, but a good percentage of females go too. John's wife, Debbie, is taking her Black belt next year.

I asked about the origin of karate, and Ged was able to show me a family tree, as it were, from the very first known person. This was a T Sacugawa who lived 1733-1815. He taught his first pupil, S Matsomura, and this carried on throughout the years until 1928, when it reached England. A man named T Suzuki came over from Japan and taught it to the British. Edgar Auckland, a Barnsley man took it up, became a Black belt and then taught it himself. Ged and John formed what became known as the Shindo-Kai Karate Association. Everyone on the family tree is a Black belt. All the names from G Burkinshaw onwards have been taught in Ged's gymnasium. 'One of the things to note', Ged mentioned, 'was that karate is a defensive sport, you should always walk away if possible'.

Quite a few youngsters go to the classes, and I asked Ged if there had been any amusing incidents with any of them. He replied 'Yes, there was. One of the mothers went up to him and said that her son was going in a competition, and she'd heard that he needed a groin box, and a gum shield, was it true?' Ged nodded his head and told her that the gum shield should be softened in a pan of boiling water, because it was made of plastic and they were very supple. Ged carried on, 'You then put it on his top teeth love, till it cools down and moulds to the shape. You've got no problem.' However, she came to him the next day and said, You know that groin box, well I put it in a pan of boiling water as you said, but when I put it on him, down here,' pointing to the lad's nether regions, 'Well, all he did was hop everywhere and wouldn't keep it on.' We all fell about at this. Ged mentioned another time when one of the young lads went up to him and asked if he wanted a sweet. Ged replied, 'Aye, I will lad.' The boy dug into his groin box and produced some Smarties. 'This is where I keep them,' he proclaimed proudly. Ged replied, 'I think I've changed me mind son.' Another time, a young lad hadn't fastened his groin box securely,and in a competition match, he shot his leg out, the box zoomed down his trouser leg, emerged and hit the referee on the head. 'I must admit,' Ged went on, 'we have some fun with the youngsters.'

I asked Ged about any trophies he had acquired, but he said that he hadn't got a lot, because of his age when he started karate. Most of his time had been taken up with refereeing.

In the beginning, karate was a bit slow to catch on, but when the Bruce Lee films came out, it fired the youngsters' imagination, and it has become very popular over the last ten years. It is a competitor minded sport, and has a very bright future. I am sure that Ged and John's gymnasium will be active for many years to come.

Some of the younger members of the Shindo Kai Karate Association exhibiting their trophies.
Centre Back: **Andy Roe (Adult) From left to right;** *Middle row:* **Lee Wagstaff, Adam Brailsford, Chris Malin.** *Front row:* **Lee Ruse, Robert Lowery, Kristian Booth, Nathan Littlewood.**

33. KENNETH SYKES

World Chamion Speed Skater and Karate Coach

THE FAMILY of Kenny Sykes' father, were very sports-orientated people. Jack Sykes and his wife, Alice, adopted Kenny when he was a baby, so it was a beautiful coincidence that he too loved sport of any description. Jack's eldest brother, Frank Sykes, was a boxer,known locally as 'The Champ'. Another relation was Charlie Hardcastle, a well-known Barnsley area boxer. Kenny could remember the family talking about them when they used to box in a marquee which used to be on the site of what is now the Barnsley bus station. Kenny was born in 1924. He said that being adopted meant that in lots of ways he benefited, because he always knew that he was really wanted and was a much loved child. When he was twelve, his parents adopted a little girl, Brenda, so completing the family.

Kenny was born at Cudworth, but the family did not stay there very long. He was brought up at Darton, where he went to the Infant, Junior, and Senior school. Kenny engaged in gymnastics, and was in the school team. Before the war, roller skating became very popular, so he started going to Wakefield Roller Skating Rink. In fact, that's where he met his future wife Margaret whom he married in 1948. Kenny's first job after leaving school was at Woolley Colliery. Mining work, together with skating and gymnastics combined to make Kenny a very fit young man. At the age of twenty, when he worked as a borer, he used to lie on his back pushing an electric drill into a coal seam with his feet. This gave him tremendous strength in his leg muscles. Five years later when Kenny was twenty five, he went in a road race from Leeds to York and back on his roller skates. He set off from Leeds Town Hall along with fourteen other men at 7.40am, and touched the wall of York Minster at 9.51am. Returning, he took 3 hours and 55 minutes, a total journey of 6 hours, 6 minutes. He was nearly three miles ahead of the second man, an eighteen year old maltster, Don Birkenshaw. Only seven men finished the course out of the fifteen starters. They tripped over cobbles and tramlines, they suffered from cramp, blistered feet, and exhaustion. In all, they covered 52 miles non-stop. All the ones who

The British Hockey Team taken in 1958. From left to right;
Back row: **Bill Cooke, Ken Stephenson, Sid Pushley, George Dyson.**
Front row: **Kenny Sykes, Johnny Gunn (goalkeeper), Len Wood.**

had not made it, came back by transport, and then they were all taken to Wakefield Town Hall by car for a civic reception. The Lord Mayor and Lady Mayoress presented the first four with pewter tankards, and all the racers received medals. Kenny held the national record for this race, sustained on one sandwich, and half a pint of tea.

This was not the only one of Kenny Sykes long distance records. He followed this by setting out on a marathon race from Wakefield to London on roller skates, accompanied by two fellow racers, Arthur Hebden, and Herbert Lund. C Wilkinson, riding a bike was the pacemaker. They reached Grantham three-and-three-quarter hours late, due to blistered feet, and continued the rest of the way by motor-cycle combination. However, the fact that they had already covered 72 miles on skates gave them the honour of the World Championship for the longest non-stop run. Newspapers at the time, stated that it was a World Record.

During this time Kenny was in the Wakefield Team, based at the *Little Bull* public house. Sadly, it was burgled in the early sixties and nearly all the photographs and trophies taken, and were never recovered. Because of his world records Kenny was asked to join the British Speed-Skating and Roller-Hockey Team. This resulted in travelling all over Europe.In one of their engagements in Germany, he saw his first pair of plastic wheels. Kenny said that it was raining and the German team could stand up on their skates much better than their British counterparts. The mystery was solved when they realised that the British Team skates were of metal and harder to manoeuvre. Kenny recalled that this was the same year as the Munich air disaster, 1958, because he still had his black armband on. Because Kenny was still working at the pit, he had to receive permission from the manager to go to events. He came back from a venue in France, and an official met him at the railway station, he said, 'I reckon you'll be off to bed now Kenny?' but the reply was, 'Not likely, I've got to go to work and do my shift now'. The outcome of this altercation was that Kenny, along with Arthur Rowe, the shot-put athlete, and Dorothy Hyman the runner, all working at Woolley were granted the privilege of time off for training and meetings, and their pay would not be deducted. This was a highly satisfactory arrangement, and Kenny was delighted.

Kenny pictured with his daughter Christine meeting Brian Roper ('Just William' fame) back in the early fifties.

When the British roller-hockey team competed in Portugal, they became World Champions. Kenny, who took part, appeared on the British Newsreel, and made guest appearances at Star Cinemas throughout Britain. He was at Belle Vue, Manchester once, and was asked if he would skate on the 'Wall of Death'. Kenny agreed, but said that it was pretty terrifying, if he hadn't got such strong thighs he would have been in trouble. Centrifugal force kept him upright, but at the end of it, the maple-wood wheels on his skates were completely worn through. It was a challenge that he would not readily repeat. Kenny used to go to Butlin camps at the weekends,teaching roller-skating and playing in the roller-hockey team. It was announced by the holiday staff, that he had been brought over at great expense from France to demonstrate his abilities, when in reality he would be bumping into his workmates on holiday, and they would all have a laugh about it. Every weekend the same trophy was presented to him by Ivy Benson, the lady band leader. This took place mainly at Filey. One little lad was so enthralled by these events, that Kenny eventually gave him his green cap. Years later, when this boy was a young man, Kenny bumped into him, he was captain of his own team and still possessed the treasured cap.

In 1965, Kenny had an accident down the pit. He was hit by a shearer rope and broke his leg in three places. This put paid to his skating career. Undaunted, Kenny carried on with weight-training and judo. By now he was a qualified instructor and taught at Darton High School, and Edward Sheerian at Athersley. Dave Blackwell, a judo instructor had taught Kenny at the *Wheatsheaf* at the bottom of Racecommon Road. Sometime after gaining his Black Belt in judo, Kenny and his friend John Lynton, landlord of the *Darton Hotel,* known as the 'Drum', spotted an advertisement in a newspaper for karate lessons. Six lessons for two pounds. The tutor was a Mr T Suzuki from Japan. He came over to England in 1962 to teach the sport, which used to be illegal in this country. Kenny said that he didn't think that there was any particular time when it was made legal, it just became a very popular sport. The lessons were held at the *Royal Hotel,* Barnsley. Kenny gained his Black Belt for karate, in fact, he was the first in Barnsley. When Mr Suzuki had to go back to Japan, Kenny teamed up with a man from Sheffield who had also been taught by him. His name was Phil Milner and together, they set up classes at a hall at Newmillerdam, followed by the Scout Hut at Darton.

By this time, Kenny Sykes had three children of his own, Kenneth,

Christine, and Steven. He recalled a time when Kenneth was a little boy of around eight or nine, and he proudly took a newspaper cutting of his father winning the Wakefield to York race previously mentioned. The headline stated, 'Dick Turpin rode to York on Black Bess, Kenny Sykes rode to York on eight little wheels'. His son said that his dad knew Dick Turpin, because they'd both travelled to York on the same day. Needless to say, the little lad was teased unmercifully by his classmates.

Kenny brought many Barnsley men up to Black Belt standard in Karate, including the World Champion Kick-Boxer, Arthur O'Loughlin. In 1983, Kenny Sykes was given some dreadful news, he was suffering from leukemia, and was confined to Barnsley General Hospital. Kenny had collapsed at work. He was given a few weeks to live, because he was so ill, but surprisingly, rallied round and spent the next twelve months in hospital care. His weight plummeted to six stone and he was given up for good at one stage.

Kenny demonstrates how to block a knife attack with the Maegeri kick. Taken in the early sixties.

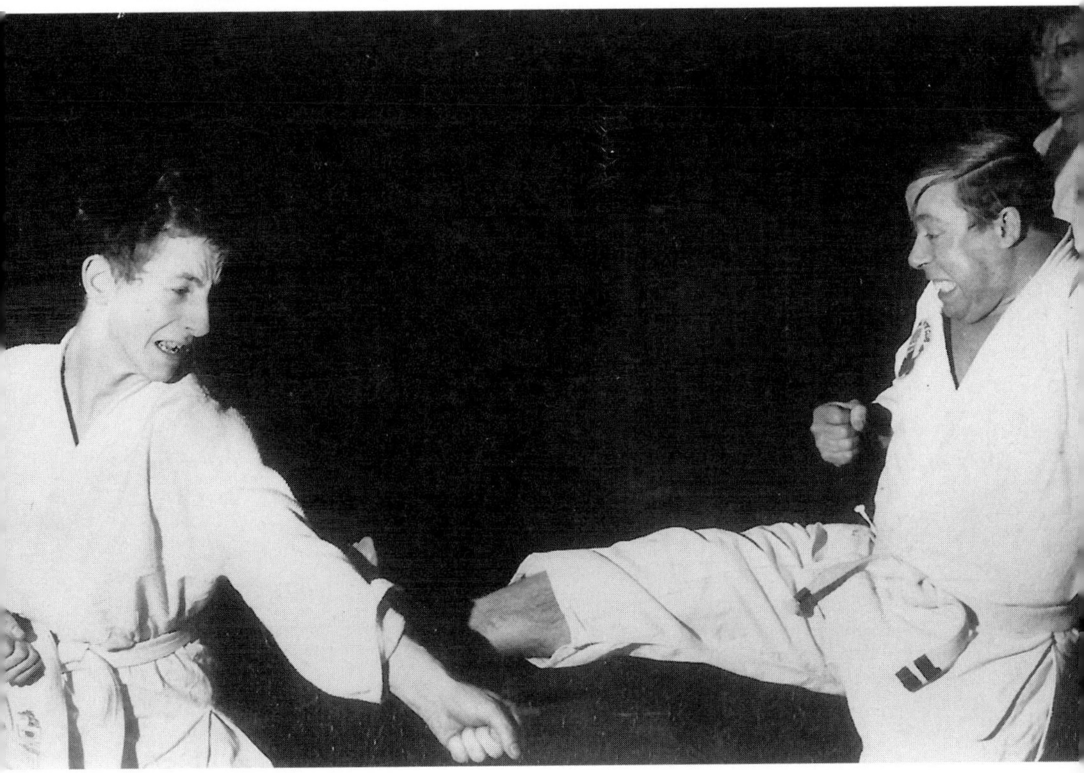

In fact, some friends thought that he had died and put a notice in the obituary column. The doctor said that it was only Kenny's extreme fitness that saved him. Ten years later, it came to Christine O'Loughlin's notice that Kenny was indeed still living, and when her husband Arthur said that he wished that he had still been around to see his achievements, she invited him to Arthur's surprise party. The old friends were re-united. It was a very happy event for them both.Kenny mischievously pretended to be a mystery contender for Arthur's World Title. He had a hood over his face, and when he removed it, his friend's face was a picture of complete and utter shock, quickly followed by joy.

During Kenny's illness, Ged and John Tumman had a plaque especially made for him. He was released from the hospital to receive it. It was in honour of all the achievements he has made in karate, and out of all his trophies, Kenny said that this was the most special. After he left the hospital to take up normal life again, Kenny Sykes was too old to enter in competition matches, so he helped to grade people. He is still great friends with Arthur and Christine, who own the Bodytone Studio at Wombwell.

Kenny is still in remission, but doesn't take life any easier. As he said, 'If I cannot have any quality of life, then I may as well be dead'. He also mentioned that when he was in one of his very darkest moments during his illness, a nun came to visit him in the night.Kenny said that he was not a particularly religious man, but she stayed about three hours, taking his hand and praying. He started to pick up the following day. 'Makes you think, doesn't it?' he remarked. Kenny is not a tall man, I am sure that he will agree with me on that score, but they say that dynamite comes in small packages, and when it comes to sheer tenacity, I am certain that Kenneth Sykes has that in plenty.

34. PETER LINDLEY

Karate Black Belt and Instructor

PETE LINDLEY was born on 20 December 1959, to Margaret and Ronald. They lived in the Pogmoor area of Barnsley, but eventually settled in Athersley along with Pete's sister, Elaine. He attended the local schools, finishing his education at St Michael's Comprehensive. It was here, at the age of fourteen, that Pete gained an interest in karate. At that time, the Bruce Lee films were showing at the cinemas and many youngsters became interested in Martial Arts. With the encouragement of his parents, Pete actually put his plans into fruition. A karate club, run by a man named Ken Waddington, was formed at St Helen's Church Hall, Laithes Lane. Pete started as a student, gaining first grade, the White Belt. Working his way to the Brown Belt, and with the tuition of sensei, John Tumman, he eventually received his Black Belt. Eight grades in all.

After Pete left school, he started work at Dodworth Colliery but

Pete and Phil Buckley sparring at the Scissett Karate Club, 1977.

when the pit closed moved to Redbrook Colliery, taking a break from karate. Pete's other love was football, so at sixteen he began training at Oakwell for the under eighteen team. He did so well that in 1977 he was made Junior Footballer of the Year. This led him to a crossroads in life, choosing between his two favourite sports. Karate became uppermost, 'But with hindsight,' Pete remarked, 'if I had stayed with football, then financially I might have been better off.'

6 October 1979, saw his marriage to Debbie, a local girl. They settled down in Athersley near to Pete's parents, and eventually had two children, Tracy and Mark. Pete entered events all over England in pursuit of his karate career. Barnsley itself, Coventry, Lincoln, Sheffield and Bradford, to name just a few. This culminated in him becoming Yorkshire Champion in 1990. His most cherished trophies are the gold and silver from this event, the British All Stars Championships held at the Concord Sports Centre, Shiregreen, Sheffield. In a match at Athersley Sports Centre, Pete sustained three

Champions of the All-Style Karate Association in full gear. From left to right: Steve Hemingway, Pete Lindley, Bryn Gray, John Tumman, John Brooks.

Members of the Shindo Kai Karate Club pose outside the *Royal Hotel* Barnsley, after collecting for charity during the Barnsley Six Race. From left to right: Bryn Gray, Pete Lindley, John Tumman, Shaun Logan, Andy Bentley.

broken ribs. He still carried on fighting and smiled throughout the photo session. Afterwards, he went outside for some fresh air because he couldn't breathe properly, fainted, and didn't wake up until he was in hospital. This little episode failed to put him off karate and on 1 August 1991, he received his treasured Black Belt. Pete, a fresh-faced young man, likes to do battle with heavier opponents, because as he put it, 'As a rule, the bigger you are, the slower you are.' He also favours team fights, saying that, 'it *psychs* me up.', He fought Wayne Otto, the World, European, British and English Champion at Crystal Palace. Pete lost, but as he said, 'It was a great experience.'

In 1994 he became the Shindo-Kai Champion. Pete has put a lot of hard work into his sport, which includes going on a week's training course to Mablethorpe where he ran for five miles every morning. At the end of the week, the organisers held a race where Pete came second. He is a registered member of the English Karate Governing Body (EKGB) and a sports coach and referee. This particular group brings all the Associations together and they make sure that the proper teaching methods are employed. Pete said that it got rid of the 'cowboys', stressing that it is so easy to damage the body and the correct training is paramount.

His life down the mines was brought to a halt with the pit closures of the 1980s. After the 1984/85 strike, Pete started work at Denby Grange Colliery but that closed too. He now works at the Koyo Japanese ball-bearing factory at Dodworth. I asked him if his son Mark had shown interest in karate. Pete replied that he had initially, working his way through to the Yellow Belt, however his enthusiasm waned and Mark just pays flying visits to training and guidance sessions now. The Barnsley Six Road Race has captured Pete's imagination, and he has entered into the spirit of it by running four times. The runners take it in turn to dress in a pantomime cow costume, whist colleagues collect money from the crowds lining the streets. It all goes to the Marie Curie Cancer Research Society, a very worthwhile cause. Pete is an enthusiastic young man and he now has his own karate school, recently taking over the premises at Darton that his friend Gary Burkinshaw has vacated. With the increasing public awareness of the expertise that he is passing on to his pupils, I am sure that the new training centre will be a success.

35. GARY BURKINSHAW

Karate Coach

WHEN INTERVIEWING the stars of karate, I have noted that their enthusiasm soars as high as their leaps in the air. This was no different when I saw Gary Burkinshaw at his comfortable Royston home. The door was answered by a smiling young man with curly blonde hair. He said, 'Just hang on a minute whilst I get the dog in it's basket'. The animal in question turned out to be an adorable little puppy, barely bigger than a man's fist. Gary put it in its bed, whereupon it promptly jumped out again. It obviously didn't realise that it was tangling with a Black Belt! Anyway, we decided to ignore it, and to talk about Gary's origins. His parents' names were Fred and Doreen, and they lived in one of the pit houses at Woolley, where Gary was born on 11 April 1964. His grandmother had moved into this long terraced row when they were first built, so Gary's family were fairly well established by the time that he came along. Gary went to the local primary school, followed by Darton High School, and then Darton Upper school, at Kexborough. In 1988, he married Fiona, and they have two children, Natalie and Scott.

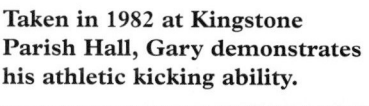

Taken in 1982 at Kingstone Parish Hall, Gary demonstrates his athletic kicking ability.

I asked Gary what had sparked his interest in karate. He replied that he had liked to watch it on television, but what had clinched it was when he was about eight years old in the Woolworth's store in Barnsley, two men in their early twenties, started bullying him. He was with a ten year old friend at the time, and the men, who had been drinking, tried to goad Gary and his friend into stealing from the store for them. Both boys refused, and Gary was hit. Upon arriving home, his parents were incensed by these actions, and his dad decided that Gary was going to learn self-defence. Fred made enquiries about karate classes and where a suit could be bought, and thus Gary started on the road to his Black Belt.

Gary's father used to take him to various classes at Scissett, Cudworth, and

Kingstone Parish Hall under the tutorship of Ged Tumman and Steve Swindle.

Gary explained to me that there are different styles of karate. *Shotokan* is an attacking kind with punching and kicking. *Shotokai* is defensive, blocking and parrying. He himself practises *Wado Ryu,* which is a combination of both. In *Wado Ryu,* Gary practises knife defences, and also studies anatomy in the higher grades so that breaks can be learned, and nerve attacks on various parts of the body, so therefore believes that this is a superior form of training. Their progression of belts is as follows: the lowest is white, followed by white with black tags, yellow, orange, green, blue, purple, brown, brown with gold tags, and then, if ready, the Black Belt. This takes roughly five years.

Gary received his First Dan in 1985. After two years, if you wish, you can then apply for the Second Dan, after three years the Third Dan, and so on.

From 1982 to 1986, Gary trained for the Yorkshire squad with all the top names. This resulted in Gary travelling far and wide with the

Darren Parr is on the receiving end of a high flying kick by Gary.

team. Amongst the venues in the home counties were Yorkshire itself, Wales, London, and countries such as Ireland and Germany, where Gary took the silver medal at Stuttgart. Reminiscing about his days in Ireland, he said that in the hotel in Belfast, the windows were covered in wire mesh, because of kids throwing bottles. There was also sniping and bombing going off. Gary smiled and said that they were known as the 'Hippo Weights', because all the team weighed around 75 kilogramme's each. Gary has always entered into team events. They were up against Alfie Lewis, the World Champion at the Richard Dunne Sports Centre at Bradford. Alfie's nickname was *The Animal.* His photograph was often featured on the front of martial arts magazines such as *Traditional Karate*, or *Combat*.

Gary watched throughout the day and observed the action. He thought 'Well, I'm not going to be scared when I oppose him'. When the actual match came, Alfie kicked Gary, but instead of blocking it, Gary grabbed his leg, *Ashi Bri'd* it and brought him to the ground. Alfie, true to his nickname, went berserk at the thought of a comparatively unknown youngster doing this to him, and particularly with all the television cameras present. This suited Gary admirably, because one of the golden rules is, 'Don't lose your head'. Alfie rushed at Gary. He in turn, sidestepped and brought him down again. Gary only needed half a point to win. This must have been seen to be abominable to his adversary, because he levelled at Gary in the air, took him off his feet, and broke his nose with his fist. This was completely out of order and resulted in Alfie Lewis being disqualified. This 'saved face', but it was a shocking way to 'cop out' as it were. As he spoke, Gary rubbed his nose ruefully, 'What a legacy'.

In Gary's first ever championship, he was an Orange Belt. It was held in Coventry, and he did so well that day that he was upgraded to the Green Belt without taking the exam. He fought and defeated five Black Belts in that particular tournament.

In 1990 Gary started his own school at Darton. He only teaches karate part-time because he has a day job. This also makes it difficult to get to championship fights, and he would like to do more. However, he finds working with his pupils very satisfying. They get enormous pleasure from learning karate, but Gary admitted that he does make them work, it isn't for the faint-hearted. Gary hopes that the youngsters will have confidence in themselves when they grow up, and that they will also be able to enjoy the team spirit that he himself has been so successful at. With Gary's technique, I think that they have a very good chance.

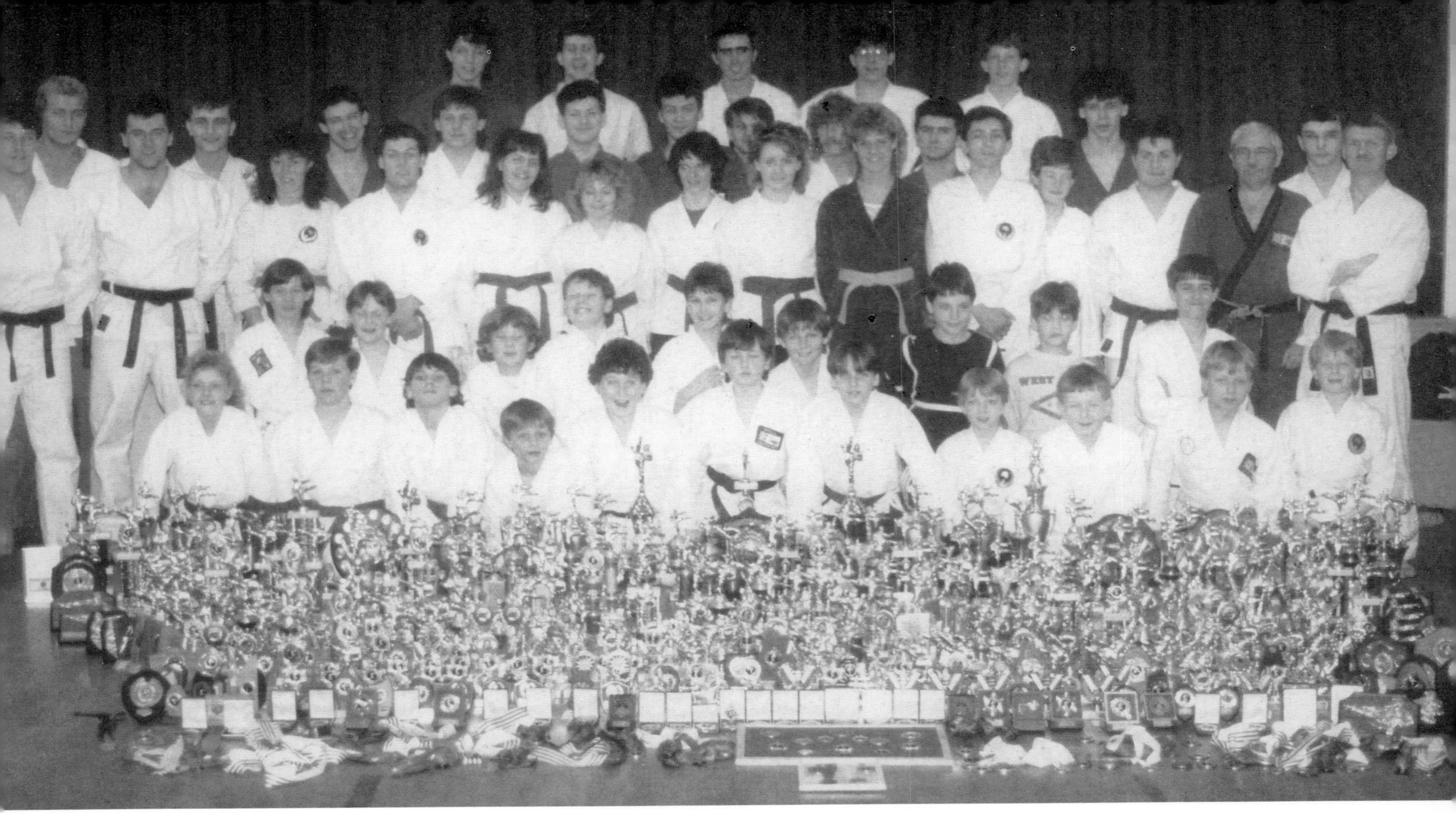

A dazzling display of trophies won by the class of Kingstone Parish Hall.

36. 'YANK' LENTHALL

Knur and Spell, and Nipsy Champion

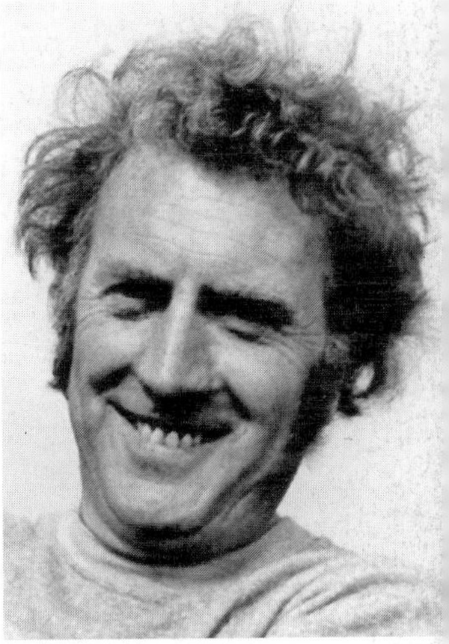

GOING TO see Frank Raynes Lenthall, was like taking a trip down memory lane. Frank, or 'Yank' as he is known by, lived two doors away from my Grandma Barrett. I too, lived in this same row of houses, Keresforth Hill Road, and have many fond memories of the games of nipsy that the lads used to play on the rough ground at Kingstone. It's the kind of sport where you need to have wide open spaces - at least we had plenty of that in those days.

Yank was born on 2 November 1934, to Elizabeth and Frank, his father was also called Yank by everyone. I never knew my own dad to call him by any other name. One of the things that always sticks in my memory was when Yank senior was passing the time of day with his mining pals outside Sergeants, a local shop, when a huge lorry careered down the hill, went out of control, mounted the pavement and trapped him. He managed to push a child out of the way, but Yank himself was very badly hurt. This happened during the 1940s. Yank did recover, but it was touch and go. The young Yank went to Agnes Road School, like most of the Kingstoners, and then to Racecommon Road.

At the age of fourteen, Yank went to his first friendly match, it was based at the *White Bear,* Worsbrough Common. He took his cousin, Harry Pearson along with him who lived on Back Denton Row. Because of their youthfulness however, they were obviously not allowed to go in the pub. When Yank left school, he worked at a couple of jobs before joining the army. Leaving in 1963, he worked in light engineering at Hoyland. During this time he married Pearl Ainsworth who incidentally played the cornet in Dodworth Miners Welfare Band, and became a very popular and well known person in her own right. She and Yank have two children, Glen and Karen. Glen has played Knur and Spell, so in effect the sport has been enjoyed by three generations.

Yank settled in Athersley, and took up nipsy seriously, winning lots of trophies along the way. At one particular nipsy match, an elderly man walked up to him and asked if he was interested in Knur and Spell. This gentleman turned out to be Joseph Edon from Dodworth Road. Strangely enough, this name had been mentioned

Frank at fourteen playing nipsy. In the background are old Kingstone houses.

to me by an old Kingstone friend, Janet Beverley. She said that Mr. Edon was a distant relation, he had been born around the turn of the century, and was a Knur and Spell World Champion.

This turned out to be true. Apparently, Joe was born near the Queens Ground, Barnsley, and this was where the game used to be played. Joe became World Champion in the 1920's. He had three sons, and a daughter. One of his sons, Stanley, sometimes played alongside Yank junior, but had to give it up through back trouble. Joe died when he was 79, the day before his eightieth birthday. Before his death though, he was quite happy to train Yank and to pass on his wealth of expertise. He also gave Yank his 'Spell', and said that it was his to keep. I looked at the fine and intricate piece of equipment on the floor, and said, 'That's a far cry from old Kingstone Yank, when you and the lads just balanced house-bricks to strike off'. Then I asked him the difference between the two sports. Yank held both sticks up. The nipsy stick was smaller and had a flat head, and the knur stick was long and flexible and the head was more of a square shape. Yank has always made his own sticks. He presses the heads with a home-made machine to condense the wood, and then shapes, carves, smooths and polishes. The type of wood he chooses is usually hardwood, such as holly, mahogany, beech privet, or Hawthorn. Yank then melts some bitumen with a blowtorch, fixes the heads onto the sticks with this solution, binds it and lets it cool.

A group of knur and spell players at the Dugdale Guinness Trophy Game taken in the 1970s. From left to right: *Back row:* **Unknown, Frank's father, Ron Darlow, Unknown, Alec Kirk, Tommy Chambers, Frank Lenthall.** *Front row:* **Nigel Flowers, Albert Mountain (referee), Glen Lenthall (Frank's son), Eric Wilson, Robin Smedley.**

As for the game itself, well a nipsy is a small oblong piece of wood, shaped and narrowed at one end. This is rested on bricks or wood, the overlay is tapped with the stick, forcing the nipsy up into the air, and then striking it. In a league match held between *The Engineers*, (Higham,) and the *The Ring'O'Bells*, (Silkstone,) Yank reached an individual score of 1,061 metres, or 1,159 yards. He received a certificate for this in 1989.

Yank then explained about the spell. The little balls known as 'potties', are balanced in the cup of the mechanism. When the catch is released, the ball soars into the air and is struck by the stick, known as the 'Pummel Head'. When playing, each man is allowed seven strokes. There is another way of playing this game which is not machine-activated. This comprises a gallows-type structure, from which the knur is suspended. It is then struck with the stick, which could be anything up to six feet long. This type of pastime has been around in Yorkshire and Lancashire for over three hundred years. Joe Edon's World record was 840 feet (14 'scores'). Yank's was 630 feet (10 'scores') when he won the World Cup in 1979. Yank won £200, and the event was sponsored by Webster's brewery. This was not Yank's longest hit. He once scored 798 feet (14 'scores'). Yank still holds another two trophies for Knur and Spell, besides the World Cup. One is the Dugdale Trophy and the other is the Calendar Trophy, given by the television programme, which Yank has sometimes starred in.

Knur and Spell has always been known as 'poor mans golf'. Yank mentioned that, sadly, the young men of today do not seem to have the same interest as their forbears. He is hoping that there will be a revival because it is such an old game, and part of our heritage. Yank also said that Mr Edon was one of life's gentlemen, and that it was a privilege to have known him. Another thing was that in those days you had to walk miles for a game, there was very little transport, so you had to be dedicated.

I played my tape back when I got home, it was punctuated by Yank's hearty laugh, a very pleasant reminder of the evening spent with him and Pearl. Let's hope that nipsy, and knur and spell will flourish for many years to come!

Frank in striking action playing the knur and spell

37. JOE EDON

World Champion at Knur and Spell

JOE EDON was born 22 March 1890, at *Queen's House,* Queen's Ground, Barnsley, now an elderly persons home. It used to be the caretaker's house for the grounds, which now hold today's modern Metrodome Leisure Centre. In the early part of this century, games of Knur and Spell were played on the fields there. The story of Joe Edon was narrated to me by his son Stanley who resides in Athersley with his wife Dorothy. Joe's parents married at Silkstone Church in 1873. They took over the *Lord Nelson,* Shambles Street, ran it for two years and then moved to *Queen's House* where Joe was raised. He was part of a large family, five sisters and five brothers. Joe practised constantly at Knur and Spell, from a very early age. He had an uncle who worked at Redfearns glass bottling plant who used to supply him with glass marbles, the type that used to be in the necks of old-fashioned pop bottles. The uncle had a billie-can that he used to fill with tea, but when emptied, could be used for the marbles. Stanley smiled, 'Dad always had a good store to draw on, they had a peggy-tub full.'

When he was twelve he made a spell, smaller than the normal size,

The Edon family taken in 1898. Joe is on the extreme left, age nine. Third from left at the back is Emily Cawthorne, sister of Joe, who tragically died twenty years later from her nightdress catching fire.

and by the age of fourteen he was a crack shot. Stanley said that his dad used to coil like a spring, a very unorthodox kind of movement, but it paid dividends and by the time he was fifteen, he was the World Champion at Knur and Spell. He also excelled at other sports. He was very good at football, playing in the reserves for Barnsley. Also, he was so good at running that he was entered in the World Championships in Manchester in 1910. Unfortunately, he beat the gun and was moved back a yard as punishment. He finished almost abreast on the tape by the winner, a South African, named R E Walker. As Stanley remarked, 'If only he hadn't been made to move back.'

Joe Edon worked down the mines before the start of the First World War. He and his brothers all joined up in the service of their country. Joe knew how to drive so he was assigned the task of teaching other soldiers. When war finished, he was asked to stay longer in order to bury the remains of English soldiers in proper graves at Flanders. The bodies had to be transferred from their shallow resting places. It was a grim task, face masks had to be worn, but it was necessary. This lasted until 1920.

Queens Ground 1910 (Queen's House is in the background. From left to right: Walter Cawthorne, Thomas Edon (Joe's brother), Trainer (name unknown), Joe Edon.

Stan aged twelve with his mother and father.

Joe came out of the army and got a job driving a wagon for Townhill's, a firm based at Worsbrough. They were contracted out to Redfearns at Old Mill Lane, Barnsley. Eventually, Joe worked full-time for Redfearns. He married in 1922, and in 1925, a year after Stanley was born, they settled at 50 Bank End Avenue. By 1930, Joe had his own wagon and taxi business to make his living from. This had been greatly supplemented by the prize money from his wins at Knur and Spell throughout the years. Unfortunately, Joe lost his title to Bill Baxter from Huddersfield in the same year, 1930. He had faced many adversaries including Jim Crawshaw, described as 'a powerful figure of a man,' but Joe's championship days were over. He still carried on playing his game, but he wasn't winning as much. Even as long ago as 1910, the stake would be £25 which were extremely rich pickings for a working class man in those days. Stanley could remember as a boy going on his push bike to watch his dad and his pal, Archie Robinson play at *The Flouch,* Hazlehead. He said that there were thousands of spectators, and he had never seen so much money change hands.

In the late forties Joe moved his family to 7 Blucher Street, Barnsley. It was also around this time that he played his last game of Knur and Spell. The house had six bedrooms, so they took in lodgers from the show business world. Performers from the *Theatre Royal,* Wellington Street used to stay at their house. Stanley has a scrap-book that used to belong to his parents, packed with cuttings and photo's about, and from, lots of their guests. I asked Stanley about his own life. He joined the Navy during the Second World War, and then after that he went back to work as a fitter at Redfearns. They were starting to make arrangements to move to a new site, the present-day one at Monk Bretton. Stanley Edon and a bottle machine mechanic, Arthur Kershaw, were responsible for helping to build the new factory. Stanley would dismantle a crane, put it on a barge, transport it by canal to the Klondyke area, put it together again and commence work on the new site. It was during the bad winter of 1947 and Stanley said that the snow was so deep that wagons were stuck up to the axles. He was putting tin on the roof when he noticed that by lunch-time the canal was just a trickle because it had burst it's banks at Lundwood.

Stanley talked about his father again. He said that he was a man of boundless energy. In fact, he showed me a cutting from the *Barnsley Chronicle* dated 2 April 1960, when Joe was 70, and trying to revive Knur and Spell. He was trying to organise a game in aid of the local Hospital's Comfort Fund. He hoped that by staging this match, then young men would take it seriously and it would become popular again.

In actual fact, this happened to the extent that it has been featured on Yorkshire Television's *Calendar*. One of Joe's willing pupils has been Frank Lenthall who too is a champion and has absorbed much of Joe Edon's teaching. In a later article, Joe said that out of a total of around 80 to 90 games, he lost only six. He once did a knock of 840 feet (14 scores) at the Queen's Ground. Joe's interest in the sport lasted until his death the day before his eightieth birthday, 22 March 1970. Stanley mentioned that his father had not been without sorrow during his lifetime. Bill, his elder brother, and Frank Stainrod Edon, the younger one worked together on the railway driving the engine. They used to have a gun in the cab so they could shoot rabbits. One day, the signals were against them at Dodworth and Frank spotted a rabbit. He walked down the track but was caught by an oncoming light engine train and it took both his legs off, fatally injuring him. Another sad episode was when Joe's sister Emily, married to Walter Cawthorne, landlord of the *Spencer's Arms* at Barugh Green, died in 1918 through her nightgown catching fire. 'There have been lots of publicans in the family,' Stanley added, 'One of them being Tommy Cawthorne, Emily and Walter's son who was landlord of the *Californian Hotel* at Staincross. He was cleaning his gun when it went off and killed him.' Their daughter Emily married the landlord of the *Talbot* public house at Mapplewell.

Joe Edon, in his latter years outside 7 Blucher Street.

Out of all the attributes that Stanley Edon paid to his father, the most outstanding were his energy, his vigour and his enthusiasm.

38. FLORENCE WRIGHT

Table-Tennis Star

I COULD NOT write about table-tennis without the inclusion of Miss Florence Wright, a star of the 1950s. She, along with a few others, helped to popularise this sport and bring it to the notice of the general public.

I knew Florence as a child at Honeywell in Barnsley. She is a relation from my mother's side, both families settling down in this area. Indeed, it was my cousin, Ken Brown, who put me in touch with Florence again, because I had lost track of her throughout the years.

Florence and her husband Jack, now live at Monk Bretton, but she was born at 95 Honeywell Street, on 4 November 1937. Her parents were named Mary Carr and Walter Wright. Florence was one of four sisters and two brothers.

She went to Beckett Street Primary school, Eldon Street Juniors, and Raley Secondary Modern. It was at the latter that she started to play table-tennis at the age of thirteen. Florence had enjoyed playing netball, but after talking to Barbara Leaf and her boyfriend, they introduced her to this alternative sport. They played for Barnsley North End Table Tennis Club which at that time was based at the *Tollgate Inn* at the bottom of Old Mill Lane in Barnsley. Barbara encouraged her initially, and then Carrie and Alan Cooke who ran the club, coached her up to the standard of playing for Yorkshire. Mrs Cooke was secretary of the Barnsley Table-Tennis League, and her husband was chairman. It was then that Alan Thompson, a player from Leeds took over for a short while, and by the time she was playing for England, Jack Carrington was coaching her. He was the British official coach to the Table-Tennis Association.

In actual fact though, before all this took place, Florence was very keen on music and singing, and she had to make the decision about which career to take. Whilst she was a schoolgirl at Raley, she appeared in concerts with the school choir. Miss Chambers was the headmistress at that time, and she used to organise these events. Florence used to sing solo, and Miss Chambers was so impressed by her, that she arranged for the Head Inspector of Music for England to come and listen to her. He broke his journey from London to Newcastle in order to do this. The audition took place at the Barnsley Girls' High School, where Florence sang, *Ava Maria, Oh*

Florence in her younger days with some of her trophies.

my Beloved Father and *Love and Music*. She also played the piano, the violin, and practised music theory.

This resulted in her being offered a place at the Royal College of Music, in London, but because of Florence's age (she was fifteen at the time), her parents would not allow it. She was then offered another place at Manchester Royal College of Music, but they still did not want her to live away from home. Because these positions were turned down, Miss Chambers became quite irate, and demoted Florence from her status of head girl, and this honour was then bestowed upon Mary Phillips, another cousin. Well at least it was kept in the family!

All this resulted in Florence turning to her other love, table-tennis. At the age of sixteen, she won the zone final of the *Daily Mirror* Girls' singles. She was playing in the Yorkshire Seconds for Barnsley North End. This led to representing the three areas, Yorkshire, Lincolnshire, and Nottinghamshire at Birmingham on 20 March 1954. She again became champion and this resulted in her competing in the National Championships which were held at the Albert Hall in London on 13 May 1954. Florence played in the quarter-finals. She was beaten, but out of an entry of 2,000 she did extremely well, and was regarded as one of the leading junior girl players in the country.

Florence was then selected to play for the England Juniors against the German Juniors at Brentford, London on 6 November 1954, shortly after her seventeenth birthday. She won her singles set, and then partnering Joyce Fielder of Kent, went on to win the doubles.

On Saturday 15 January 1955, Florence made her third appearance for the Yorkshire First Team against Gloucestershire, thus qualifying for her premier division badge, and becoming the first Barnsley player to receive such an honour. Altogether, she won county recognition 22 times, and was twice Yorkshire's closed women's champion and three times open girl champion.

I asked Florence exactly what she got out of the sport, and she replied that if it hadn't been table-tennis it would have been something else that was energetic, because that was her nature.

In 1957 at the age of nineteen, Florence married Jack Rollings, a

Florence showing her two sons David and John a thing or two about table tennis.

miner, and retired from table-tennis. In the years following, they had two sons, David and John. Florence became a hairdresser, and settled down to family life.

After a gap of five years, at the age of twenty-four, Florence decided to make a comeback, having a strong desire to play the game again. She was accepted back and it wasn't long before Florence was playing for Yorkshire again, but although still an extremely good player, lacked the dedication of her youth and retired permanently a year later. Florence carried on hairdressing, twenty years in all, but she said at the end of the day there was nothing better than taking the make-up off, letting the hair down, and playing sport.

Florence and Jack's two sons are both sports-minded, but have settled for ordinary jobs in a stable environment. As she said, 'the only prizes in table-tennis, or indeed in any amateur sport are cups, or everyday objects, such as table-lamps. Expenses would be paid, but in reality a dependable job is needed with an employer who understands when time off is required to pursue a particular sport.

I asked Florence what her interests were today. She answered with a smile, 'I enjoy the company of my four grand-daughters, I walk every day, and I play badminton and squash.' This I can believe, because she looks very fit and has kept her slim figure. Florence achieved many honours in her sport and can look back at her sporting achievements with pride.

39. BRIAN AND EILEEN STARKIE

Table-Tennis Champions

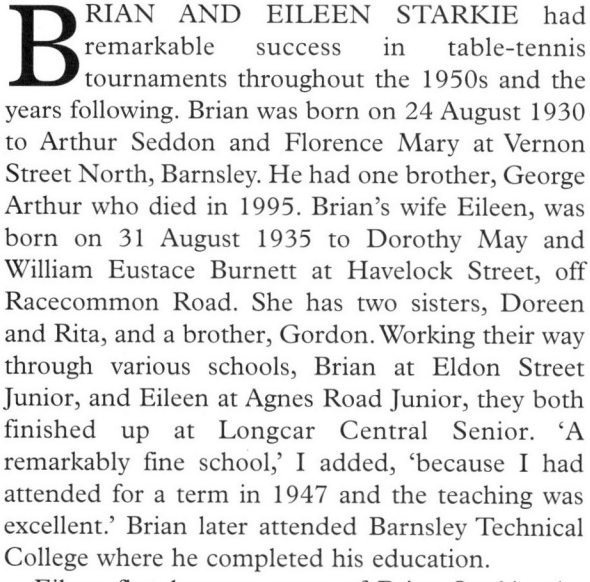

BRIAN AND EILEEN STARKIE had remarkable success in table-tennis tournaments throughout the 1950s and the years following. Brian was born on 24 August 1930 to Arthur Seddon and Florence Mary at Vernon Street North, Barnsley. He had one brother, George Arthur who died in 1995. Brian's wife Eileen, was born on 31 August 1935 to Dorothy May and William Eustace Burnett at Havelock Street, off Racecommon Road. She has two sisters, Doreen and Rita, and a brother, Gordon. Working their way through various schools, Brian at Eldon Street Junior, and Eileen at Agnes Road Junior, they both finished up at Longcar Central Senior. 'A remarkably fine school,' I added, 'because I had attended for a term in 1947 and the teaching was excellent.' Brian later attended Barnsley Technical College where he completed his education.

Eileen first became aware of Brian Starkie, the man who was to be her future husband, when he came to play table-tennis at Racecommon Road School Youth Club. She was invited by him to go to Raley School Youth Club and participate in the events. Brian remarked that Harry Ogley was a source of encouragement in those early days, also a player named Jim Birkett. 'In fact,' Brian said, 'Thirty years on, I got around to telling Jim that I had styled myself on him.' Eileen laughed, 'Better late than never.' They started courting each other and in 1952 were married.

Eileen's first important table-tennis match was the Yorkshire Junior Open Girls' Singles. She won a fashionable mock-crocodile handbag and could barely contain her excitement when going home to tell her mother. Her job at the time was sewing collars at the local shirt factory. Brian worked as a cable jointer for the Electricity Board, a job which he pursued for 46 years. He also did National Service in the Army as a young man. Upon his release, he joined forces with Geoff Williams and Colin Barker, and the trio played for

Raley in the Third Division of the Barnsley League. In their first year they were runners-up. In the Grade B Men's Singles, Brian went on to beat Fred Scarfe in the Finals.

When Brian was 21, he could no longer enter the Youth Tournaments so he joined a variety of other clubs, amongst them, the Wanderers and Barnsley YMCA. He first represented Barnsley on 25 March 1952 in the Yorkshire League. He played in the second team in the men's singles at Doncaster, winning both matches. On 4 November of the same year, Brian made his first team debut against Leeds seconds. He won one game, but lost the other, playing away.

A group of finalists pose at the Broadway Youth Club in the late 1970s. The men's and women's Barnsley Championship finals were won by Brian and Eileen (centre).

He and Eileen had many wins in the run up to 1963, when they formed their own club, the Ace. Joining them were Geoff Williams, Trevor Lyon, Mildred Mosley, Mick Fieldhouse and Terry Ballinger. The year following, Dave Gascoigne and Betty Till entered their services. The club was not a great success however because it was hard finding suitable premises for them to play in.

By now, the Starkies had three children, Melvin, Christine and David. Another child, Neal, was born fourteen years after their last child. The first three entered tournaments along with their parents, and in 1969 the whole family walked away with awards at the Barnsley Table-Tennis Championships. Eileen won her Grade B singles trophy against George Partridge (NALGO), with much vigour and determination, the score being 24-22. This was followed by the mother and daughter team, Eileen and sixteen year old Christine, beating Miss Valerie Liddall and Mrs Pauline Williams in the Ladies Doubles final, the score being 21-12 in the final set. Eileen partnered her husband Brian for the Mixed Doubles against her former opponent Valerie Liddall again, and Alan Hydes, the England International. Again, they formed a formidable team, winning the third important set with a score of 21-18. In the Junior Singles their youngest son, David, aged 12, carried off the trophy, beating his finalist brother, Melvin in the process. Altogether, the Starkie family took away five trophies that particular night.

Another big moment for Brian and Eileen was on 25 March 1975 at Broadway Youth Centre, when they won the coveted singles titles in the Barnsley Table-Tennis League Championships. Brian also won the veterans' trophy. It was a very proud moment for them both to win in the same year. In 1962, Eileen was teamed with Lillias Hamilton in the final of the East of England Ladies' Doubles Championships at Butlin's, Skegness. Leslie Bell and Elsie Carrington were their opponents, both women being No.1 seeds. It was an exciting finish with Eileen and Lillias winning the third and final set, 22-20. A month later in Manchester, Eileen played Lesley again in a single's match. It was described on the radio, 'The blonde 'bombshell' from Barnsley beats Lesley Bell.' Eileen described this as her highest achievement.

'Talking of holiday camps,' Eileen remarked, 'we don't seem to do so badly. I was once 'Pontin's Ping-Pong Princess.' Eileen went on to explain that even though she and Brian retired from playing table-tennis in 1983, they would still enter for fun when they were on holiday. She became 'Champion of the Week' in 1992 at Seacroft Holiday Village in Norfolk, receiving an inscribed trophy and a voucher. 'Another time,' Brian added, 'we were on holiday at the Isle of Arran on the West coast of Scotland in 1984'. They were at a village where they were holding a festival that week called 'Corrie Capers.' There were table-tennis competitions going off so the Starkie family joined in, this time with their youngest son, Neal. He won 'tea for two' at a nearby hotel, Eileen came third with a small prize, and Brian won a voucher for £10 which he used to buy an LP. Eileen smiled, 'It made a change from trophies.'

Brian Starkie has appeared for Barnsley 276 times, a remarkable achievement which will probably never be beaten. He and his wife Eileen have also both made 100 representative appearances in the Yorkshire League for Barnsley. They have gained much pleasure from their chosen sport and have raised their children in the same beneficial way. As Brian added, 'Table-tennis was played in the spirit in which it was intended. It had a happy atmosphere, and for his family, it was a way of life'.

40. SAM BETTS, ALIAS DWIGHT J INGLEBURGH

Boxer and Wrestler

SAM BETTS is an old Kingstoner, so as soon as I saw him and his wife Sheila at their home in the Stairfoot area of Barnsley, I recognised familiar faces. Sam was one of three survivors of ten children born to William and Theresa Betts. The other two were his sisters Mary and Jessie. Sadly, Mary died a few years ago. They were all born at 10 Keresforth Hill Road, close to the old *Bush Inn*. I distinctly remember the house, because nearly all the properties had about nine or ten steps leading up to the front doors, and we kids used to run up one flight, jump about a foot across to next door's steps' and back down the other side, sometimes giving a knock for further annoyance. Sam laughed, 'So it was you Annie'!

After we reminisced for a while about Kingstone, I asked Sam

'Nobody move, or Dr Death gets it.' Sam demonstrates his power at Butlins in 1958.

how he had managed to enter the wrestling world. He replied that it all started from a boxing booth at Dodworth fair. Sam, who was born on 13 March 1933, strolled along to the fairground when he was ten years old, and volunteered to fight in a boxing match. The proprietor of the travelling booth, a ' Professor Boscoe,' wanted two young lads to fight for half-a-crown each, (12.5p), a decent amount of money for a youngster in those days. They had to wear boxing gloves too. Young Sam put up a good show and became fired with ambition. He was at Agnes Road Junior Boys' School, but on the verge of entering Racecommon Road Seniors. By the age of twelve, Sam was boxing at the Boys' Club, then based along Wellington Street, Barnsley. The man who trained and encouraged him was Bob Archer. At fourteen, Sam joined a gymnasium at Quarry Street run by Charlie Glover, the father of Brian Glover, famed actor and wrestler. It was here that Sam and Brian, trained under the expertise of Charlie and two other men, Jimmy Birch, and Reg Leybourne. By this time Sam had added wrestling to his curriculum too.

Sam left school at fourteen to work at Barnsley Main Colliery, and then left for another pit. After a couple of years, he switched jobs and worked at Fox's Steel Works, Stocksbridge. He was still training throughout, but the lease on the Quarry Street gym ran out and Sam then did his training in a room above the stables at the back of the *Fitzwilliam Inn,* Sackville Street. Eventually, Charlie Glover took over some rooms at the rear of the *Junction Inn,* Doncaster Road (Reg Leybourne's sons' run it now). Sam was called upon to do his National Service when he was eighteen. He was delighted with all the facilities available to him, and finished up in the army boxing team. Sam started off as a light welter-weight at 10st 4lbs, but by the time he left he was fighting as a 14 stone heavy-weight. He had blossomed out into a mature young man. During his army service, he was stationed at Chelsea Barracks, the home of the Irish Guards, most of his duties being on public guard outside Buckingham Palace

After Sam Betts left the army in 1953, he rejoined Her Majesty's Service a year later, but this time it was to be the Merchant Navy, a life on the ocean wave. He took his weights along with him for training purposes and built up his body a bit more. In 1956, upon his release, Sam returned to Barnsley and trained at his old gym for a while before travelling around England with a mobile boxing booth. This was a return to Sam's grass roots, and his first love. He toured all over the country to such places as Devon and the Nottingham Goose Fair. The ring would be set up, and the punters would throw their loose change, called 'nobbins', into it. Sheila laughed and said,

'He used to have about ten fight's a day, and come home with bags of pennies'. Sam added, 'I believe that it was about 1956, when the Government eliminated entertainment tax, which made it possible for the wrestling world to pay more'. This encouraged Sam to take up wrestling professionally.

He was known in the trade as 'Dwight J Ingleburgh'. This was one of Brian Glover's brilliant ideas. Sam said that Brian was most inventive when it came to choosing pseudonyms. 'Because let's face it', he added, 'there is an element of show-business in wrestling, and it has to be entertaining.' Brian chose this particular name for Sam because Sam had travelled on the *Queen Elizabeth* when he was in the navy and Brian thought it would be a good idea to pass him off as an American. I asked Sam who 'Doctor Death' had been, the mystery man who always wore a mask. He chuckled at this, and said that all he and his circle of wrestling friends had been Dr Death at some time in their career.

In 1960, Sam and Sheila were married. They have four children, Sam Junior, Joanne, Danny and Samantha. Incidentally, Sheila herself is a talented lady. She writes poetry in the Yorkshire dialect, has helped with the Talking Newspaper for the Blind, and is at present working on her mother's life story.

In 1967, Sam went to wrestle in India. The money there was very good at that time,'But there again,' he added, 'the wrestlers were huge men, and you were literally fighting for your life'. If one of the villages had a man suitable for wrestling, then he would be feted. The

Karachi, 1974. Sam *(third from left)* **wins the Pakistan mid-heavy-weight title.**

inhabitants would see to all his requirements, even if they were poverty stricken, because it was a huge honour to have recognition brought to the village. Their rules in the wrestling game were fairly lax, they wanted their man to secure a win by fair means or foul. When Sam was in Bombay, about 20,000 people attended to watch youngsters fighting in the sand. This started about 10 o'clock in the morning, and carried on throughout the day in searing heat. In the evening, the star wrestlers appeared and fought in a proper ring. By this time, the crowd numbered around 70,000. Fighting was still held in the open air at night-time because of the heat. The money for these events was quite good, £200 per week, and all found. Sam added, 'We couldn't earn money like that in England, and it was only for two fights a week as well'.

He remembered one fight in Kashmir though, when the crowd started to turn nasty. Their wrestlers were also film stars, and were treated like gods', and Sam was defeating their hero. In the end big Sikh soldiers stepped in, and said 'We protect you, Sahib'. They started to escort Sam to a local army barracks, but the crowd were still in a vengeful mood. Sam enquired as to what they could do, and the soldiers said, 'Pray for rain, Sahib'. Sam was predicting a sticky ending, when unbelievably the rain poured down, the crowd dispersed, and Sam breathed a sigh of relief.

Another bad moment for him, when in India, was the start of the five-day Egyptian War. He had to fly back in a TWA plane full of wounded Vietnam war veterans. He recalled the very bad shape that they were in. Upon Sam's return to England, he went on the normal wrestling circuit, six nights a week. In 1973, he fought in Singapore, Malaysia, and Kuwait, alongside his old friend, Jack Land. Wrestling has left Sam with numerous injuries and arthritis, but as he said, he wouldn't have changed anything. His career lasted from the age of ten, to forty eight. He has also worked for British Rail for twenty five years until his retirement in March 1993. All in all, a very active man.

Sam still likes to keep fit – with gardening, and working out in a small gym that he has installed for himself at the back of the house. He has taken one or two young men under his wing, including Steve Savage, who has done very well in the body-building business. Sam junior, also runs his own gym at Kirkham, near Blackpool. He went in the army at sixteen, and like his father, boxed at different weights. He finished up as light-heavy-weight champion of the British Army. Sam Betts, senior however, can now rest on his laurels, after enjoying a very satisfying career.

41. JACK LAND, ALIAS KRAMER VON KRAMER

Boxer and Wrestler

JACK LAND, has had a long and varied career. He and his wife Betty welcomed me into their Kendray home. He is a thoughtful, genial man, and she, a spirited lady with a bubbly personality.

Jack was born at 3 Grace Terrace Barnsley. The town's old abattoir was at the bottom of the street. His parents were named Harold and Mary, and he was born on 1 April 1930. He went to school at St John's, Barnsley, but his parents, trying to better themselves moved to Bradford. Unfortunately, Bradford was bombed in 1939 so they returned to Barnsley.

Harold Land bought a fish and chip shop. The entrance to the shop was in Duke Street, and the house entrance was in Thomas Street, but as Jack recalled, 'The biggest attraction was being so close

Jack in prime condition in his early boxing days.

to the 'Bugs Hut', the *Star* picture palace on Brittania Street.

Jack first started his sporting career at the age of twelve whilst he was still a schoolboy at Racecommon Road Seniors. He trained in boxing at the *Vaudeville Club,* Shambles Street. Apparently, it was an old club which supported drinking, but didn't have a licence, so there was a police raid and the place was closed down. Charlie Glover, the father of Brian Glover, the well-known actor, took it over and turned it into a gymnasium. Jack trained there for a while and then the gym was transferred to the bottom of Quarry Street, off Doncaster Road. Boxers trained in the upstairs room and wrestlers were downstairs.

Eventually, they all moved again to a building at the back of the *Junction Inn,* Doncaster Road, where it still is today, but under different ownership.

When Jack was fourteen, he left school and worked on the screens at Monk Bretton Colliery. Besides boxing, he had a keen interest in football, playing for local teams. Jack was boxing in the National Coal Board Championships, but this was curtailed by the accidental death of a close friend whilst working down the mine. Jack was at Woolley Colliery at this time, but he was so sickened that he left mining and joined the Army Cadets. At sixteen he was the Army Cadet

Jack pictured here with wrestling star, Massambula. Sadly, Massambula's career was curtailed when a misjudged body slam left him an invalid.

Champion, but this was then followed by National Service.

Encouraged by his wins, it was the ideal moment for Jack to further his career. He was fighting as a middleweight by now, at 11st 2lbs. Jack was in the Duke of Wellington's Regiment, stationed near York. He developed a suspected mastoid and was hospitalised and his weight shot up to eighteen stones. The mastoid was cured, but Jack then had the problem of losing his excess poundage. Upon returning to the barracks, he put an inner car tyre around his middle, a thick sweater on top, and wore heavy boots. He then skipped, down in the boiler room. This, combined with early morning runs, and playing in the football team, soon brought his body back into condition.

Whilst still in the army, Jack was invited to box for the Police Club in Minden, Germany. He accepted, and boxed their champion who at one time had been in the Olympics. Jack won after three rounds, everyone was shouting 'Prima, Prima'. He was presented with a large bouquet of flowers and the referee whispered, 'Split them in half and keep yours and give the other half to your opponent'. Apparently, it was an old custom, but Jack was pleased to do as he was asked. This win resulted in him adding the BAOR German middleweight title to his Battalion title.

After leaving the army in 1952, Jack worked at Robinson's Flour Mill in Rawmarsh, and whilst playing for the Parkgate Welfare Soccer Team, he was invited for trials to play for Sheffield Wednesday. This gave him the honour of playing in the same team with such as Albert Quixall and Derek Dooley. After a short time though, Jack returned to his first love, boxing. He came back to Barnsley and took it up again, but after one or two impromptu wrestling sessions he decided that he was going to switch careers and take up wrestling. He

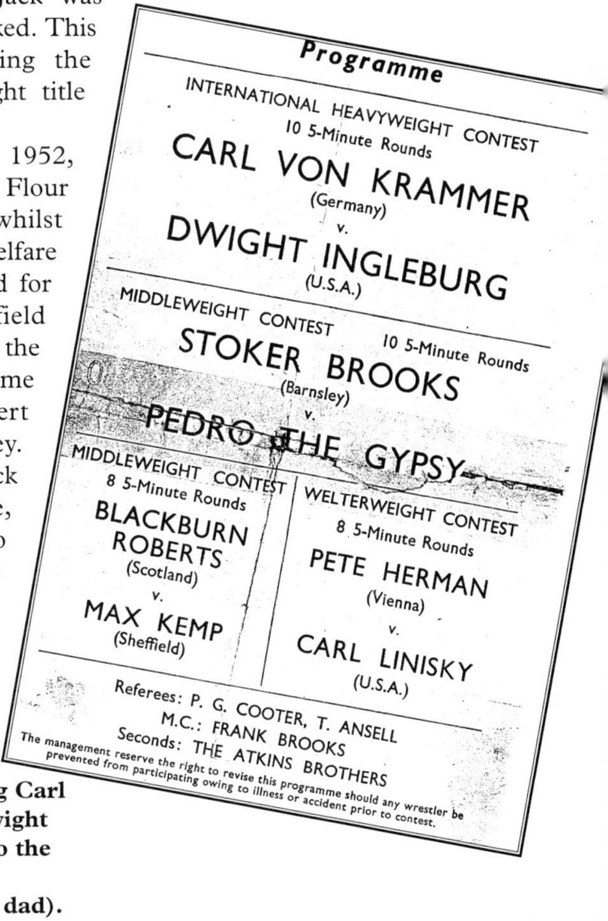

Programme

INTERNATIONAL HEAVYWEIGHT CONTEST
10 5-Minute Rounds

CARL VON KRAMMER
(Germany)
v.
DWIGHT INGLEBURG
(U.S.A.)

MIDDLEWEIGHT CONTEST
10 5-Minute Rounds

STOKER BROOKS
(Barnsley)
v.
PEDRO THE GYPSY

MIDDLEWEIGHT CONTEST
8 5-Minute Rounds

BLACKBURN ROBERTS
(Scotland)
v.
MAX KEMP
(Sheffield)

WELTERWEIGHT CONTEST
8 5-Minute Rounds

PETE HERMAN
(Vienna)
v.
CARL LINISKY
(U.S.A.)

Referees: P. G. COOTER, T. ANSELL
M.C.: FRANK BROOKS
Seconds: THE ATKINS BROTHERS

The management reserve the right to revise this programme should any wrestler be prevented from participating owing to illness or accident prior to contest.

An old programme featuring Carl Von Kramer (Jack Land), Dwight Ingleburg (Sam Betts), Pedro the Gypsy (Gordon Allen), Carl Linskey (Christian Linskey's dad).

went under the name of *Kramer Von Kramer.* This was due to a German wrestler not turning up one night, so Jack used the title instead. He also teamed up with Brian Glover and they formed *The Toffs* (later, Butch Goodman took over). Their outfits consisted of black tights, black vests, dickie-bows, tail-coats, and top hats, whilst balancing trays of crystal drinking glasses in their hands!

I asked Jack if anyone else in the family had boxed or wrestled. He said that his older brother, Dennis, had boxed professionally with old timers such as Sid Tune and Tony Hardcastle. Jack turned professional wrestler in the late 1950s. He fought at home and abroad and won many bouts over the years. He was a tough act to follow.

His family are still in the public eye, because his daughter Betty and her husband Tony Noble tour the working men's clubs as *The Midnight Duo.* They are a striking looking couple and are well known in this area with their singing act. Jack also has two sons who have shown an interest in football. The eldest, John, played for Huddersfield from the age of fifteen to eighteen. His position was left full-back. The younger son, Carl, plays for the *Cutting Edge* soccer team based at Worsbrough. At the present time, they have won their league matches for the last two years running.

Jack has kept himself fit and only retired from wrestling at the age of 65. I asked him if he had any final thoughts about his sporting life. He said, 'Yes, it had been a way of living in a sport that he enjoyed, and that he had travelled the world and had a much fuller life than he might have had normally'.

42. GORDON ALLEN, ALIAS 'PEDRO THE GYPSY'

Wrestler

ONE OF THE first things to strike me about Gordon Allen the well known wrestler, or to give him his professional name, 'Pedro the Gypsy', was his inborn sense of humour. He's a big jovial man with iron-grey curly hair. I could imagine his stage name being very apt in his younger years.

Previously, Jack Land, a fellow wrestler and old friend of his, rang Pedro to say that I would be calling to see him. He said to Jack, 'Ask her to fetch some fish and chips on the way, not too much salt and vinegar'. In my naivety I whispered to Jack, 'Which fish shop does he like? Jack handed me the phone, and all I could hear was Pedro's (as he likes to be called) booming laugh, 'I'm only kidding love'. This set the tone for my interview with him at his home near Locke Park where he lives with his wife Jean. She used to be a 'clippy' (bus conductress) many years ago, working on the 'Trackies', so was in the public eye quite a bit herself.

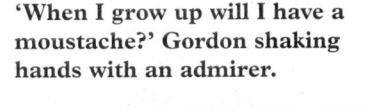

'When I grow up will I have a moustache?' Gordon shaking hands with an admirer.

Pedro was born in Beech Street, Barnsley, on 23 July 1924, to John and Blanche. He attended St Joseph's Junior School, and Holy Rood, confiding that he used to be an altar boy. When his schooldays were over, the young Pedro took up weight-training. His father John, used to be a boxer and encouraged his son in these activities. Apparently, he too was a strong thick-set individual with a fifty-two inch chest. Pedro had a variety of jobs up to the age of nineteen when he took up wrestling. He had a little gym of his own at Buckley Street, at the back of a shop where coal was sold. The rent in those days was four shillings a week, inclusive of water, electricity, etc. After this , he trained at the *Junction Inn* on Doncaster Road.

Meet the Rock Chords. One of the many rock and skiffle groups that sprang up in the fifties. From left to right: Brian Panks, Gordon Allen, Barry Gooder, Geoff Almond.

He won his first match at Ilkeston, Derbyshire, against a man called Granville Lawrence from Pogmoor. When wrestling became popular at the holiday camps, Pedro went on the circuit with opponents such as Jackie Pallo. Pedro also remembered a time when he got 'chinned'. Touts were selling tickets to see Randolph Turpin, the boxer, at Aberystwyth. After Randolph had lost his middleweight title he took up wrestling. Pedro squared up to him and said tauntingly, 'It's not Sugar Ray Robinson you're fighting now lad'.Turpin's answer to this was to give him a left hook which sent him across the ring and through the ropes. Pedro was dazed, but stood up and resting his chin on the floor of the ring, 'Just like Chad', he looked up at his adversary and spluttered, 'Randy, I will not be coming back'.

Pedro was cruiser weight in his heyday, and has wrestled in Germany, Finland, Sweden, Tenerife, Denmark and America. He was known for his humour in wrestling. In a match at Harwell, near Abingdon, he was drawn to wrestle with Kevin Connelly from Ireland. At one stage, when he was holding Connelly down, he turned his opponents palm uppermost and remarked, 'You've not got long to live, according to this'. Connelly turned the tables by practically de-bagging Pedro in an illegal move, but he was still allowed the winning fall. Running alongside Pedro's wrestling career, he did some extra's work in films and television, appearing in, for example, *The Railway Children, The Water Babies* and *Crown Court*. Show business in the Fifties gave Pedro and some friends the idea of starting a Rock'n'roll and Skiffle group. The groups' other members were Brian Panks, Geoffrey Almond, and Barry Gooder. They called themselves, *The Rock Chords*.

Bobby Barron, a wrestling promoter and one of the 'bad' boys of wrestling.

One of the saddest memories that Pedro can recall, was when an old wrestling friend, Arthur Betton from Warren Quarry Lane died. Arthur used to fight under the name of 'Butch Goodman'. He finished up in a wheelchair suffering from motor neurone disease. Pedro said that it broke his heart to see him die with this wasting illness after they had seen such good times together. Pedro himself had a heart attack at the age of 68 after a wrestling bout at Skillington Club. This was closely followed by another, so he decided to call it a day and retire. Even this didn't dampen his spirits, he mentioned that he hadn't been able to see the Golden Gates, because his scrap merchant friend had got there first. Nowadays, Pedro is confined to watching wrestling on satellite television. He is tinged with a little sadness that his own glory days are gone. As he said, 'It's in the blood'.

Pedro left me with the feeling that he's a hard nut with a soft centre. Incorrigible, but a genuine bloke. As I was departing, the phone rang, Pedro's voice drifted through, 'We can talk now, Yorkshire Television's just leaving, they wanted Jean but she's not in, so I wore her frock'. What did I say? Incorrigible!

43. CHARLIE GLOVER AND SON, BRIAN

Boxers, Wrestlers and Entertainers

(Dedicated to Brian Glover)

CHARLIE GLOVER was a well-known Barnsley boxer. He was born around 1890 and as a youth became interested in the fight game. Like lots of sporting pit-men around that time, he was very talented and fought all-comers. A good description of him was written by Ben Green of the *Green 'un,* in 1956:

> *Charlie Glover, a self-styled pit-man's champion of the North was a light-weight who took part in over four hundred contests. A fair percentage of these were for side-stakes that reflected his confidence in his own prowess, and what is more, he always won when the money was down. In the early 'twenties', Charlie's services were in great demand. and I recall one period when he won as many as forty-five*

'We'll get thee reight lad.' Charlie Glover and Jim Birch tend to a boxer (unknown).

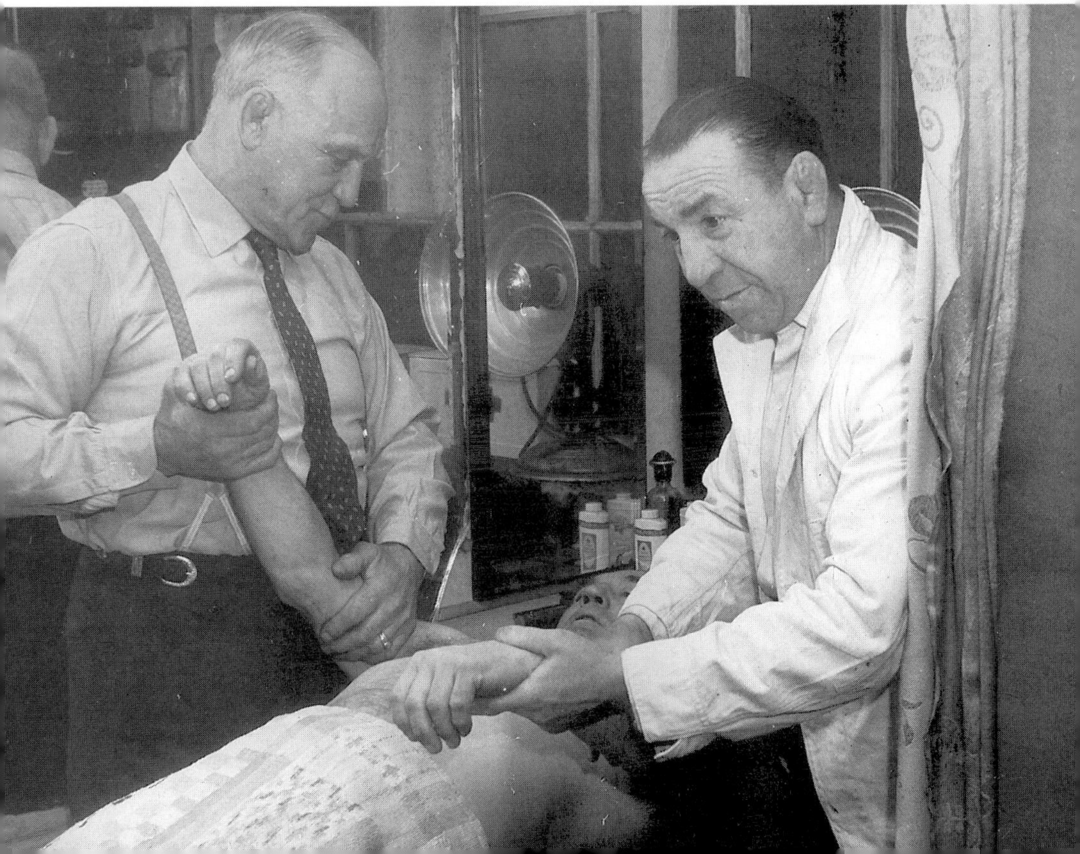

contests in a row.

The most notable thing about Glover was that he was always ready and willing to take on all comers any time and anywhere. If the money was down he demanded a weight of 9st 9lb with a give-or-take clause of two pounds. For any other contest he would never quibble at giving from four to seven pounds away. He could box or fight, dish it out or take it, and it made no difference to him whether the distance was 10, 15, or 20 rounds.

Two men he met several times were Tom Mallinson (Leeds) and Charlie Fletcher (Glossop). They had decisions given against each

Charlie posing with boxers, Jack Gardiner and Frank Walshaw.

other, but whatever the result, they knew at the end they had been in a fight in which no quarter had been asked or given. They met several times at the Leeds NSC and elsewhere, and you could always depend on a great contest and a packed house wherever they were billed. The three of them knew every trick of the trade, but it was usually a case of thrills galore. When I think of the repertoire of punches, feints and shifts they produced, I say quite seriously, that I never came across boxers in the whole of my career who had a greater variety of armaments than these three. Although they usually looked sorry sights at the end of their contests, I honestly believe that they enjoyed every minute of the fights.

Ben Green went on to say that Charlie Glover's fights were far too numerous to mention, but ones in particular were contests with Billy Forest, Jimmy Baker, 'Kid' Eastwood, Arthur Abbott, Willie Gilmore, 'Curly' Murphy, Andy Newton, Tommy Gray, Jack Dunn and Jim Hall, all inside the scheduled distance; and with Scotsman Willie Devanney whom he beat on points over fifteen rounds

Junction Inn taken from Cemetery Road side. The gymnasium is to the left at the back of the yard.

Charlie formed his own gym at the old Vaudeville Club, Shambles Street. He then transferred it to rooms at the bottom of Quarry Street, off Doncaster Road, and eventually finished up at the back of the *Junction Inn*, Barnsley. This gym is still there today, run by Graham and Stephen Laybourn. He fought his last fight at the age of 51, after which he began

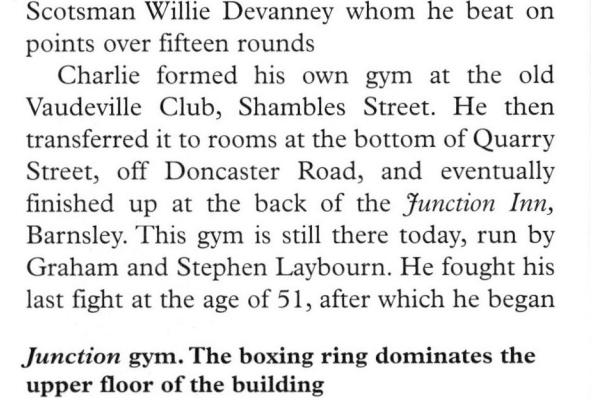

Junction gym. The boxing ring dominates the upper floor of the building

training other boxers and wrestlers. At one stage in his career, he was assigned to coach Jack Gardner, who was then the former British, Empire and European heavy-weight champion. Jack had beaten Bruce Woodcock for the titles in 1950. When Charlie became Jack's trainer, he was 65, and his protégé was 30. It was said that Charlie Glover looked like a man twenty years younger, and with the energy and stamina to match.

Charlie Glover's son Brian, born in 1934, is a household name. This is due to his appearances in film, television and on stage. Before this ever happened though, Brian was following in his father's footsteps as a wrestler. He fought under the name of Leon Arras, but also appeared with Jack Land as 'The Toffs,' until Butch Goodman took over. Sam Betts, another friend of Brian's, said that they would often have to take over as 'Doctor Death,' if the original had not turned up. Both Sam, Jack and Gordon Allen ('Pedro the Gypsy'),

You'll need a pot on your arm when I've done.' Joe Edwards (Barnsley's crockery merchant), in a clinch with Harry Hutchinson at the *Junction* gym.

spoke about their wrestling days with Brian. Many bruises were sustained but there was good-natured competitiveness about the business.

When interviewed by Rosanna Street, author and free-lance journalist, Brian described his early days as a wrestler:

> *I used to teach in Barnsley and on a Friday I'd finish at four, go to Leeds, catch the five o'clock plane down to London, get a stand-by to Paris, be in the ring that night and then go on to Basle for a fight the next day. On Sunday I'd fly back and be in Barnsley at half past ten at night. People would say, 'Where've you been this weekend?' I'd say, France and Switzerland, and they'd say 'Bloody liar.'*

In wrestling mode. Brian's wrestling career far out-shadowed his boxing past.

Brian initially combined his teaching career with his wrestling. He taught French and English to Barnsley schoolchildren. Although Brian was born in Sheffield, he was raised in Barnsley and married a local lady, Elaine. They had a daughter, Maxine, but the marriage was dissolved in 1974. He and his present partner, television producer Tara Prem, have been together for twenty years and have a fifteen year old son named Gus. Before all this however, Barry Hines, a teacher and colleague of Brian's, wrote a book, *Kestrel for a Knave,* about a Yorkshire boy and his pet kestrel. The book was turned into the film, *Kes,* Brian Glover playing the part of a bullying games master. This classic film resulted in a turning point in Brian's career. He was snatched up for many other roles, leaving teaching and wrestling behind in favour of professional acting.

Brian is well-known for his smooth, billiard-ball head and muscular figure. It gives him a tough look for some of the characters he plays. Returning to Brian's interview with Rosanna, he decided how his appearance had been modified by the 'fight-game':

> *I was disfigured by wrestling. I am quite a good looking fella really. I was knocked ugly, I'm not really bald. My hair was dragged out by irate men trying to take advantage of my pristine body.*

It's obvious from this quote that Brian possesses a sense of humour, a true Yorkshire-man, very much tongue-in-cheek. He enjoys living in London however, having lived in the same two bed-roomed flat in Chelsea for the last twenty-five years. The view from his kitchen window spans St Paul's, Crystal Palace and Harrods. After *Kes,* Brian did a season with the Royal Shakespeare Company, playing in *Richard II* (in Stratford and New York), *Romeo and Juliet, The Taming of the Shrew* and the part of 'Charles the Wrestler' in *As You Like It.*

Since then he has played roles from Soviet leader Khruschev, to God, and has written and produced twenty plays. He has appeared in hit movies such as *Brannigan* with John Wayne, *The Great Train Robbery,* with Sean Connery, *Aliens 3* with Sigourney Weaver, and the award winning British film, *Leon The Pig Farmer.* Amongst his television success's have been *Minder, Porridge,* and gay wrestler 'Selwyn' in *Anna Lee.* My own personal favourite, though, was a play which centred around Brian and a few male friends booking into a guest house for a deep-sea fishing holiday. They never did achieve their desire for oak-smoked kippers for breakfast, the landlady saw to that. A very good story, beautifully written. Many people will have also recognised Brian Glover's voice-overs in the Tetley Tea-bags advert, and Allinson's, the bread 'wi' nowt taken out.'

A very positive person, Brian has given the public a great deal of pleasure and has lived life to the full.

"The death of Brian Glover, at the age of 63, occurred during the publication of this book. I did not meet him personally, but he corresponded with me by telephone and letter. I sent him the finalised script and he wrote to me, 'well done, well researched, and great to read about my father again.'

He was a true definition of a Yorkshireman, Barnsley can be proud of him and he will be sadly missed."

44. WILSON'S WONDERS

by Keith Lodge

No publication paying tribute to the sporting heroes of Barnsley would be complete without reference to the remarkable achievement of Barnsley Football Club in winning promotion to the top flight for the first time in its 110-year history.

It is a feat that should not be undervalued. For not only was it historic for the club itself, it was also quite extraordinary in terms of football generally.

While rivals spent more than a million pounds on one player, the entire Barnsley team which clinched a Premiership place with a 2-0 home victory over Bradford City on April 26, 1997, cost less than that.

The most expensive signing was striker John Hendrie for £250,000; then came Neil Redfearn at £180,000; Arjan de Zeeuw at £50,000; Darren Sheridan at £25,000; and Martin Bullock (£15,000).

The vast experience of Paul Wilkinson and Neil Thompson was obtained for no fee at all, and David Watson, Nicky Eaden, Andy Liddell and Adrian Moses emerged as the truest local heroes, having progressed through the youth team ranks after being discovered locally.

Two of the other more costly acquisitions, Mattie Appleby (£250,000) and Steve Davis (£180,000) were out injured on that memorable day, leaving Peter Shirtliff (£120,000); another free transfer, Jovo Bosancic; and Clint Marcelle, who was bought in for a nominal fee, on the substitute's bench.

In that context alone the fact that Barnsley Football Club earned the right to join the country's elite for the first time was little short of a miracle.

That the capacity crowd which packed Oakwell for that final spine-tingling home game could celebrate the best football in the division, as well as promotion, was also an achievement at which to marvel.

It was, indeed, very much like watching Brazil all season, as the fans took to singing. Pass and move; create space; push up in support; comfortable on the ball; organised defence; an ability to switch effortlessly from one formation to another; individual

Above: **Nicky Eaden, Mattie Appleby and Martin Bullock celebrate after the Reds clinched promotion to the Premiership with a 2–0 win over Bradford City.**
Below: **The Champagne flows for David Watson, Arjan de Zeeuw and Neil Thompson**

trickery; and the Three Musketeers' principle of teamwork – all for one and one for all.

All this reflects great credit on manager Danny Wilson, who was the mastermind behind the fairy-tale success story. When he arrived at Oakwell as assistant-manager to his old friend Viv Anderson on the departure of Mel Machin in the summer of 1993, his performances on the pitch did not exactly endear himself to the Oakwell faithful at first, and he took a lot of stick from the fans as he struggled to adapt to the different demands of the First Division after years in the premier grade.

He was honest enough to concede that he was not playing well at the time, and admitted that the supporters had good reason to criticise, but he quickly won them over, and the following season those very fans who had pilloried him voted him as their 'Player of the Year'.

By this time he was also manager, having taken over when Anderson left to join Bryan Robson at Middlesbrough. He said then:

> *We want success. We don't want to stay in the First Division. We want to go up. But to do that we need to bring quality to the club so that we can compete on equal terms with clubs who are buying big. It could be that success will come this season, but it may take longer. Our aim is to produce good football right the way through the club that fans can enjoy watching.*

Success did take a little longer, but not much. In his first season the Reds missed out on the promotion play-offs on the last day; in his second they faded in the run-in to finish just above mid-table. But in his third the dream was realised and by playing the kind of football he had promised at the outset.

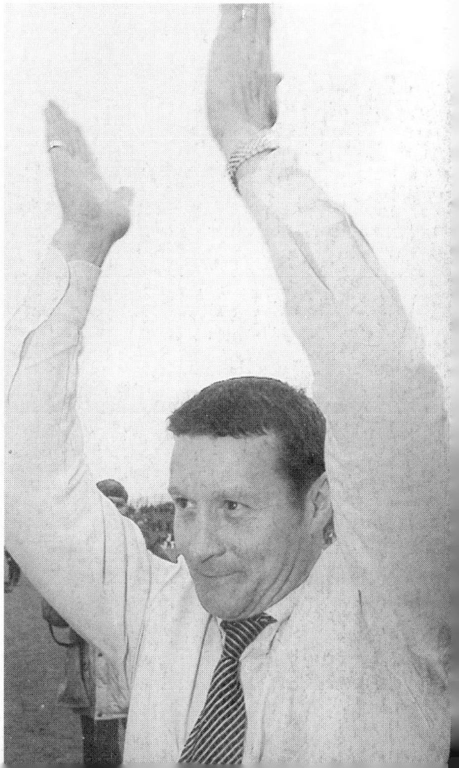

Daniel Joseph Wilson is no stranger to success. After spells with Bury, Chesterfield, and Nottingham Forest, where he learned an awful lot under the managership of Brian Clough, despite the fact that he played for the first team only ten times, he did well for a while at Brighton, and even better on joining Luton Town, who were involved in three cup finals during his three seasons with them – Simod, Littlewoods and Mercantile Credit.

The success story continued when he joined Sheffield Wednesday, with promotion to the old First Division and a Wembley triumph in the Rumbelows Cup in his first season; Europe in his second; and two cup finals – FA and League – in his third, although the latter brought the double disappointment of defeats by Arsenal.

He knew after the first game of the 1996-97 season against West Brom at The Hawthorns that his Barnsley side were capable of winning promotion. The Reds produced some scintillating football to triumph 2-1, despite the fact that there were five new players – Jovo Bosancic, Mattie Appleby, Clint Marcelle, Neil Thompson and Paul Wilkinson – in the side. He reflected:

It was a game which left me full of optimism. The way the new players immediately gelled was a massive bonus for us, and I knew that we could only improve as the understanding between them developed. I was even more convinced after winning our first five matches. That run was the catalyst. The players themselves developed a confidence and stature as the season progressed. They also had the bottle when it mattered.

But it was Wilson himself who must take most of the credit, and the Manager of the Year accolade bestowed on him by his fellow managers was no more than he deserved. He is indeed one of Barnsley's great sporting heroes. Despite the fact he was born in Wigan!

The other heroes who made up Wilson's Wonders during that memorable campaign were goalkeeper David Watson; defenders Nicky Eaden, Steve Davis, Adrian Moses, Mattie Appleby, Peter Shirtliff, Arjan de Zeeuw, Neil Thompson and Scott Jones; midfield players Neil Redfearn, who was also captain, Jovo Bosancic, Darren Sheridan, and Martin Bullock; and strikers Clint Marcelle, Andy Liddell, Paul Wilkinson and the supporters' Player of the Year, John Hendrie.

Barnsley FC's Division One promotion winning side 1996-97. *Back row (left to right):* Malcolm Shotton (reserve team coach), Eric Winstanley (first team coach), Peter Shirtliff, Steve Davis, Adie Moses, Paul Wilkinson, David Watson, Adam Sollitt, Laurens Ten Heuvel, Arjan de Zeeuw, Neil Thompson, Andy Liddell, Colin Walker (youth team coach). *Front row:* Mick Tarmey (physio), Mattie Appleby, Clint Marcelle, Darren Sheridan, Scott Jones, Martin Bullock, Danny Wilson (manager), Neil Redfearn (captain), Nicky Eaden, Jovo Bosancic, John Hendrie, Paul Smith (physio).